Turkey at the Straits

A SHORT HISTORY

By

JAMES T. SHOTWELL
and FRANCIS DEÁK

New York

THE MACMILLAN COMPANY

1941

TURKEY AND THE STRAIT

Zones demilitarized by the treaty of Lausanne (1923)
Railways

Miles
0 50 100

R O M A N I A
Bucuresti (Bucharest)
Danube
Ruse (Ruschuk)
Shipka Pass
Pleven (Plevna)
B U L G A R I A
Plovdiv (Philippopolis)
Constanța
Varna
Burgas
Edirne (Adrianople)
(U.S.S.R.)
Crimea
Sevastopol

B L A C K   S E A

GREECE
Thasos
Samothraki
Imroz
Limni
Mytilene (Lesbos)
Khios (Chios)
Ikaria
Samos
A E G E A N   S E A
Cyclades
Los (Nikaria)

İstanbul
Üsküdar
Sea of Marmara
Bandırma
T U R K E Y

İzmir (Smyrna)
Afyon Karahisar
Eskişehir
Ankara (Angora)
Konya (Iconium)
Adana
Kayseri
Sivas
Trabzon (Trebizond)
Erzurum
Mt. Ararat
Van

A R M E N I A
GEORGIA S.S.R.
Batum (Batum)

Dodecanese
Rodi (Rhodes)
Candia
Crete

M E D I T E R R A N E A N   S E A
Cyprus (to Gt. Br.)

S Y R I A
Aleppo
İskenderun (Alexandretta)
Mosul
I R A Q
M E S O P O T A M I A
Euphrates
Tigris
to Baghdad, Persian Gulf, & India
to Beyrouth, Damascus, Mecca, & Medina
to Egypt & Suez

Inset

GREECE
BULGARIA
Chatalja
Tekirdağ (Rodosto)
San Stefano (Constantinople)
İstanbul (Constantinople)
Üsküdar (Scutari)
Bursa (Brussa)
Mudania
B L A C K   S E A
S E A   O F   M A R M A R A
Gelibolu (Gallipoli)
Çanakkale (Chanak)
Tenedos
İmroz
Samothraki
A E G E A N   S E A

Miles
0 10 20 30 40 50

J. Pauw

PREFACE

". . . The war has made us all unduly weary of diplomatic tangles. The guns have cannonaded the whole Victorian façade of Austrian, Russian and German diplomacy into political rubble. The Constantinople problem of the seventies is as interesting to us as that which faced Byzantine Emperors."[1] In this striking phrase, written at the close of the World War, the Lord Chancellor of Great Britain consigned to academic cloisters a page of history which then seemed—relatively—closed. Meanwhile, other guns have spoken, and the page is once more open. Weary or not, we must turn to it again, for the question with which it deals is not to be got rid of by our ignoring it, as recent events have shown.

To at least half of Europe there is no other single international problem of greater importance than the control of the few short miles of waterway that connects the Black Sea with the Mediterranean, those narrow Straits which separate Europe from Asia. While it was not until the end of the eighteenth century that control of the Straits became a matter of interest for Great Britain, the strategic importance of Constantinople was throughout its history based as much upon the control of shipping as upon the territory over which it ruled in Asia and Europe. The power and influence which the metropolis of the

[1] From Lord Birkenhead's review of Lady Gwendoline Cecil's *Life of Robert, Marquis of Salisbury*, in *The Times*, November 18, 1921.

v

Near East maintained from the day of Constantine to that of Kemal Pasha are something which the western world has never properly appreciated. Passing over the stretch of a thousand years of medieval history during which Byzantium remained a citadel of culture, we find the Turkish Caliphate at the dawn of Modern Times extending its conquests over subject populations as far into Central Europe as the fringe of the hills by Budapest, and even breaching the walls of Vienna. After the great days of Venice and Genoa, its fleets dominated the Mediterranean until their defeat by Don John of Austria at the battle of Lepanto. But the Caliphate was more than a great power; it was a symbol of the impact of the Orient upon Europe—a symbol of which the whole Mohammedan world was conscious. For centuries the call of the muezzin at Saint Sofia was heard from Senegal to India. But when the static East was brought into the theatre of western commerce by the opening of the new seaways to the Orient, the ancient routes that centered in the bazaars of Constantinople ceased to serve as vital connections between Europe and Asia.

The decline of Turkey was inevitable. But the question of the Straits acquired a new significance with the rise of Russia, reaching down to touch the ports of the Black Sea. The vast continent of the Slavs, rich in resources and manpower, was bound sooner or later to be more than a mere source of supply for Mediterranean peoples, as had been the case in Ancient and Medieval Times. Yet, it was only in the nineteenth century that Russia, like Great Britain, fully awakened to the importance of having a free window on the Mediterranean as well as on the Baltic. Thus Turkey found itself in possession of the strongest strategic point in that long stretch of buffer territory which separated the two great European nations that were rivalling each other in Asia: the land-power of Russia and the sea-power of Great Britain.

At this juncture the new industrial Germany appeared, with its ambition to control the overland route from Berlin to Baghdad, one vital link of which lay across the Bosphorus, from Constantinople to Scutari. The old caravan trail across Asia Minor was to be revitalized. It was a plan which apparently had much to commend itself to Turkey, not only for its economic possibilities in opening up the old Ottoman hinterland, but also for the political advantage which it offered in bringing Germany into the diplomatic strategy of the Straits at a time when Russia and Great Britain had composed their differences in the Triple Entente with France.

The peace settlement which followed the World War attempted to introduce a wholly new chapter in the history of the Straits by the open recognition of the fact that it was a question of international interest and should be removed from the atmosphere of intrigue and latent diplomatic hostility which had characterized it in the pre-war years. But the theory had not reckoned with the new vitality of a Turkey resurrected under Kemal Pasha. The Great Powers were forced to admit once more, as in the times of the great caliphs, that Turkey itself assume leadership in the determination of policies that center at the Straits. How far this new orientation will go is a problem to which history offers no clue, for the new developments in Turkey have no parallel in its past. But so long as Turkish nationalism shows the broad vision of world affairs which has marked its policies in these last years, the return of the control of the Straits to Turkey is not a step backward to reactionary policies but a recognition of the new nation's right to the inheritance which it has taken over from its predecessor, conferring upon her that kind of trusteeship which makes trade an instrument of peace and uses a strategic advantage as a public utility.

As recent events indicate, the drive on Constantinople and the Straits is by no means over. Indeed, so long as international relations are based upon the politics of power, the question of the Straits will remain a recurring challenge to statesmanship. Although at the moment it is still far removed from the theatre of war, a new struggle for control of the Balkans and for the gateway to the East began at the outbreak of the present war and has been gaining momentum steadily. The mutual assistance pact concluded between Turkey and the Western Allies in October, 1939, the steady growth of Turkish influence on the Balkan peninsula as clearly shown by the Belgrade meeting of the Balkan entente in February, 1940, are merely evidences of the vital importance, both strategic and economic, of this narrow waterway in European diplomatic history.

From this short summary it will be seen that the pages which follow pick out only a single theme from the confused history of the Near East, that of the control of the Straits. Even within its own restricted field it offers no more than a guide to the principal chapters in diplomatic history and to the pertinent documents in each case. The narrative has been reduced to the simplest of outlines so as to keep the perspective clear of detail. At the same time the reader will find in the notes and bibliographical guides the necessary references for further exploration in history and international law. As for the division of our task, it may be of interest to state that the first half of the volume, the text down through the Congress of Berlin, is drawn from a memorandum prepared in 1918 as part of the documentation of the American Commission to negotiate peace at the Paris Peace Conference. It was published in 1921 in an International Conciliation pamphlet of the Carnegie Endowment for International Peace. The second half of the volume, by Professor Deák, carries the narrative down to the present moment. It thus has been possible for him to connect the problems of history with those of the present moment.

CONTENTS

CONTENTS

TURKEY AT THE STRAITS

I

ANCIENT AND MEDIAEVAL PERIODS

GREEK PERIOD

THE "Question of the Straits" is one of the oldest and most persistent problems in European history. It dates from the dimmest antiquity of Greece: the myths of Jason and the Golden Fleece—which were not all myths. From the very first it showed its twofold aspect, commercial and strategic.

The political issue of the Trojan War, in the thirteenth century B.C., was the control of the Dardanelles. The frail craft from the Mediterranean, working their way slowly against persistent northeast winds and the strong current of the Hellespont (Dardanelles), were easy victims for those who held the stronghold on the southern shore into which they were apt to be forced to turn for supplies. The power of Troy was erected on this strategic-economic fact. Forcing the Greek sailors to halt there, it brought down to its own bazaars the raw materials and produce of the rich Black Sea trade. The remains of many cities before Troy, on the same hill commanding the mouth of the Dardanelles, show that beyond the dawn of history the control of the Straits enabled those pre-Trojan and Trojan predecessors of the Turks to reap rich harvest of market tolls and dues in about the same way the Turks have profited in modern times.

Agamemnon, leader of the Greek entente, finally cleared the waters for Aegean ships to reach the source of supplies instead of stopping at the Trojan entrepôt.

This was a larger fact in the development of ancient Greece than the historians appreciated, for history in the antique world paid little attention to economics. But in the period of Greek expansion, when colonies were planted throughout the Mediterranean, an important part of the movement was toward the Black Sea. Of these settlements less is known than of those of the west, on which early Roman civilization was so largely based; but they were a more intimate part of the Greek economy, for apart from the products of the farms of Thrace they tapped the Oriental trade routes in their harbors along the dangerous southern coast of the Black Sea, and they brought grain and gold from the posts along the northern shore.

Yet, as Thucydides reminds us, the commerce of the Greeks did not amount to much before the ascendancy of Athens. Their ships were small and frail, merely enlarged row-boats, mostly unprovided with upper decks, and carrying their cargo in the open. Until the battle of Salamis, Greek sea-power was insignificant. The Persian army of Darius could cross the Straits and ravage European territory with impunity; and Xerxes could throw his bridge of boats across the Hellespont from Abydos, almost at the very spot where the British garrison in 1922 stood waiting the onset of the Turk from Asia. After Salamis, sea-power asserted itself. The ships of Athens grew in size to be the Majestics and the Normandies of that date, and the mistress of the Aegean made it a cardinal point in her policy to hold the Black Sea route both by her fleet and by colonies and dependencies along the Hellespont. At the narrows of the strait she had two colonies, facing each other, Sestos on the Gallipoli peninsula and Abydos at Nagara Point on the Asiatic side. Thus she controlled the trade of the Euxine, which flowed uninterruptedly to Athens until the Athenian empire was destroyed by Sparta in the Peloponnesian War. The story of that long struggle is the subject of the greatest work of antique history; but few readers of Thucydides are led to realize that the crowning blow which ended Athenian supremacy was that final sea-fight on the Hellespont itself, when the Spartan fleet won the day at Aegospotami. When the grain trade was cut off, there was nothing left for Athens but surrender.

ROMAN PERIOD

The control of the Straits was clearly a vital matter for the sea-going Greeks, centered in the Aegean. The interest of Rome in Mediterranean trade lay rather in the south and east, in Egypt and Syria. It collected its toll on the Black Sea trade at Abydos on the Dardanelles; but it was also in control of other more important routes to the Orient. The fundamental point, however, was that, by the time it had reached the Euxine, it had no rivals to exclude. After sea-going Carthage had been destroyed and Pompey had swept the eastern Mediterranean of those free-booting traders whom the Romans viewed as pirates, the maritime as well as the land empire of Rome was universal. For many reasons, too, the gate to the Oriental trade lay through Egypt and Syria rather than by the Black Sea; while the grain of Africa and other more readily accessible parts of the Empire reduced proportionately the importance of that element so vital to Athens. It is therefore evident that there could be no "Question of the Straits" under the Roman Empire.

A new era began, however, with the division of the Empire at the close of the third century A.D. The capital which Diocletian chose for the eastern world was Nicomedia, now Ismid, on the south-eastern gulf of the Sea of Marmora. Already the center of gravity was shifting to the Straits when Constantine the Great in 330 chose the site of old Byzantium for his new capital. The reasons for the founding of Constantinople were primarily political and strategic rather than commercial, since it lay like a fortress at the ferry on the land route between Asia and Europe. In Constantine's day it was these land routes, and not the sea-ways, which held the Roman world together. The naval engineers had no such triumphs to record as those who built the Roman roads. But in the succeeding years, when the barbarians broke through the outlying defenses on the frontiers and cut the line of march from east to west, it was the maritime strategic value of the city that held so well the key to the eastern seas, which kept the name of Rome a symbol of empire in the East until 1453. For Constantinople, planted as a fortress and a political capital, became a port and a commercial city—the only great port which kept alive the traditions of antique culture during the dark ages. This rôle it owed in part to the strength of its walls, which time and again defied the invader, but also to its fleet, which was able to control the Straits much more successfully than its armies the surrounding provinces.

Byzantine Period

The rise of Mohammedanism in the seventh century, cutting off western Asia from Europe, did not destroy the advantages which its unique position gave to Constantinople. On the contrary, it tended rather to accentuate those advantages. For while the fleet and its engineers were able to foil the Saracens in 673–677 and again in 718, the fall of its rivals, Antioch and Alexandria, gave the Black Sea route once more something of the significance which it had held for the Greeks of the Aegean. The city itself developed that mixture of Greek, Roman and Oriental culture known as Byzantine, and, even under degenerate rule, was able to draw sufficient vitality from its commerce to rival the splendor of the lords of Asia. Its strategic position was such that it did not fall to the Turk until long after he had swept beyond it and held Europe to the Danube.

It was not the Moslem, however, but the trading cities of Italy who forced upon Byzantium the "Question of the Straits" in its mediaeval form. In the eleventh century these cities, especially Pisa, Genoa and Venice, won their way across the Mediterranean by defeating the Mohammedan corsairs, and began their career of commerce. Reaching Constantinople, they sought for their merchants' privileges, as foreigners, of marketing and of free passage beyond to the ports of the Black Sea. But each city sought them solely for itself. There was no idea of an "open door" in mediaeval commercial theory. And commercial exclusiveness in foreign markets was reflected in political history at home; in constant war and mutual destruction.

The chief rivals at Constantinople, the Pisans, Genoese and Venetians, were constantly at war. The great stroke of Venice was to turn the fourth crusade against the Greek Empire itself, and hold the city from 1204 to 1261, from which time it assumed an overlordship of the Black Sea, forcing both Pisa and Genoa to accept its terms. But the Genoese had their revenge when they helped the Greeks to recover their capital, and received as reward, in addition to the confirmation of their commercial privileges, an exclusive control of the Black Sea trade. All enemies of Genoa—meaning mainly Venice—were to be denied the ports or markets of the Empire. As a result, Genoa pushed its trade on the Euxine and its colonies—of which Caffa, emporium of slaves (Slavs) and Oriental produce, was the most important—and formed a sort of colonial dominion on the northern and eastern shores.

The details of the Byzantine period lie outside the scope of this history, but it is interesting to note that through it all the conflicts which these policies of commercial exclusiveness engendered spread back to Europe and led to long disorders. The development of Italy, and, with it, of Europe as a whole, was retarded for centuries by the struggle of the jealous states of the Mediterranean to seize, each for itself, the monopoly of markets and the control of seas which, had they been open, would have brought prosperity to all.

The question of the Straits was obviously a European question from the beginning of European states.

II

THE TURKISH RÉGIME

THE CLOSURE OF THE STRAITS

THE conquest of the Straits by the Ottoman Turks was a gradual one, extending over a century. Their predecessors in Asia Minor, the Seljuk Turks, whose rise in the eleventh century was one of the chief causes of the Crusades, had suffered both from civil war and from the Mongol invasion so that the Greeks in Byzantium were able to maintain even their feeble hold on the Asiatic shore. But in the closing years of the thirteenth century the chieftain of a new band of war refugees from central Asia, Osman I —whence the name Osmanli or Ottoman—carved out for himself a new sultanate, the foundations of which were laid by defeating the Greeks of Byzantium, so that he could reach to the Sea of Marmora. His son Orkhan, after the conquest of practically the entire southern coast of the sea and straits, profiting from Greek dissension and treachery, sent an expedition across into Europe about 1350, under his son, Suleiman. Finding the country open to him, Suleiman finally crossed the Dardanelles and seized and fortified Gallipoli in 1356. From that time, with but slight intervals, the Ottoman Turks have held the fortifications on both sides of the Dardanelles, which at this point are only about a mile in width. Meanwhile they proceeded with the conquest of the hinterland, overrunning Thrace and establishing their capital in Adrianople in 1367.

For almost a century after the Turks had taken the ports on the Dardanelles, Constantinople still held its own against the apparently inevitable fate. The explanation of this anomaly is not to be found in any heroic mood or religious fervor of crusade upon the part of the Greeks, but rather in the general international situation which the passage of the Dardanelles by the Turks had brought about. For the Italian traders were now genuinely concerned with Turkish policy, as they had formerly been—and still continued to be—with Byzantine. So Genoa by diplomacy (1387), and Venice by war (1416), won from the Turks the concession of a free Dardanelles. It was a precarious freedom, but so long as sea-power remained to the Genoese and Venetian fleets, the possession of the land fortifications was not enough to secure the control of the passage. That had to await the invention of heavy artillery.

It was not at the Dardanelles but at the Bosphorus that the Turks finally established their control of the Straits. It should be recalled that the closure of the former presents an entirely different problem from the closure of the latter. The Dardanelles could be opened to Christian shipping, by special grants to European states, in order to reach Constantinople. But the Bosphorus holds the key to the Black Sea. Turkish control of it was a first step in the taking of Constantinople. The year before the capture of that city the Turks built a fort of great strength on the European side of the Bosphorus, opposite the one which had long stood on the Asiatic side just at the narrowest point— about a mile wide—where the current is strong and navigation most difficult. And in this tower of Roumili Hissar, whose picturesque and massive ruins still guard the Straits, Mahomet II planted heavy cannon, at last made available through the services of a Hungarian founder, and forbade any vessel to pass without express permission. Constantinople, cut off from the east and practically shut off from the west, soon yielded to the assaults of a sultan who was also an engineer. The control of the Bosphorus by the cannon of Roumili Hissar became permanent.

The Genoese at Galata were at first granted privileges by the Turks similar to those they had enjoyed under the Greeks, and for a while they were allowed to pass the Turkish Bosphorus forts upon payment of a toll, but ships attempting to pass without halting were fired upon and sunk if they refused to stop. The Black Sea trade was thus brought to the verge of ruin. So long, however, as the Turks did not control the shores of the Black Sea as well as the Straits, they did not exclude all Christian shipping from the Straits. That control was not established until 1475, when, having already overrun the southern, western and eastern shores, the Turks took Azof and Crimea, reducing the Tartars to accepting their rule and ending the career of the old Genoese colony at Caffa. This made the Black Sea a Turkish lake, and, for the next three centuries, until the arrival of Russia in 1774, it was the settled policy of the Ottoman Empire to exclude all foreign ships from the "virgin waters" of the Euxine through the closure of the Bosphorus.

The rise of the Ottoman Empire in the fifteenth and sixteenth centuries is one of the major events of history, the significance of which is yet not fully appreciated by those who supply the school histories for western European or American readers. The period which seems to the average student to be fully given up to Renaissance, Reformation and religious wars was also the period of the advent of an empire which was perhaps the greatest the world has seen since Roman, or at least since Saracen, days. Just when Martin Luther was launching his revolt Selim I (1512– 1526) extended his empire by conquest over the Persians and the whole of Kurdistan, Syria and Egypt. Master of the sacred cities of Islam, he forced the last of the Abbasid caliphs to surrender to him and his successors the title of caliph and the outer symbols of that sacred office, the holy standard, the mantle of the Prophet, and—not least—his sword. His son, Suleiman, or "Solomon the Magnificent," with the heritage of Asia at his command, sent his hosts into the Danube Valley. In 1521 he captured Belgrade and in 1526, at the Battle of Mohács, defeated the Hungarian King Louis II, who perished with the flower of his chivalry. A creature of the Sultan was enthroned at Budapest, whose rocky escarpment by the Danube still bears the marks and memories of the Turk. Vienna was next besieged, but without success (1529), and Suleiman's advance to world-empire was stayed. Even as it was, he reached and ravaged Styria and Carniola, almost at the gate of central Europe. At the same time his corsair admiral, Khair-ed-din—known to the Christians as Barbarossa—established his power in Northern Africa and spread terror in the Mediterranean.

By a strange turn in events the best friend of Suleiman in Europe was the one who, by age-long traditional policy, should have led in the coalition against him. Francis I, however, beaten to his knees by Charles V, was in no mood for a joint crusade upon his rival's other enemy. Much had changed since the days of St. Louis. But even yet the historian must be cynical who is not shocked to find that it was emissaries of the King of France who were sent to stir up Suleiman to march upon the Hungarians on the fatal field of Mohács.[1] Francis chose, however, to follow this policy through; and finally, in 1536, the Caliph and the "Most Christian King" made a treaty which laid a basis for French supremacy in the Levant.

The exact substance of this treaty and its bearing upon the question of the Straits is discussed in the following section. But before turning to it we should recall the economic as well as the political importance of this new policy to France, that of friendly *rapprochement* with the Turks. The consolidation of the Asiatic Empire of Selim and the conquest of Egypt had at last brought the entire Oriental and East Indian trade into the monopolistic hands of Turkey. The conquest of Constantinople in 1453, while it must have injured this trade with the west, did not do so effectively, for the other ports were still open, especially Alexandria. The greatest splendor of Venice, indeed, is in the half-century following the taking of Constantinople. It was able to tap the other routes, and generally remained on sufficiently fair terms to bargain with the Turks. It was this advantage which France now prepared to share. But another event had already robbed the Levant of its unique commercial value for Europe. For in 1499, Vasco da Gama had found the sea-route to India and the flow of trade was diverted from Cairo to Lisbon, sufficiently, at least, to ruin Venice. Thus, while Spain and Portugal and later Holland and England turned to the rich profits of sea-borne trade, France reaped no such harvest from the

[1] Cf. Lavisse, *Histoire de France*, Vol. II, p. 50.

agreement with the Turk as would have fallen to her had the world remained mediaeval and limited to Mediterranean channels for its outlet to the east.

It would carry us too far afield to follow these suggestions further, however, and we must return to the narrower problem of the effects of this new turn in events upon the trade of the Straits and the Black Sea.

The Capitulations

The treaty of Francis I with the Sultan is the starting point for the study of Turkish international relations with the states of western Europe. In addition to grants of religious and political privileges under French consuls—to which are to be traced the French claims to protect Christians in Turkey—foreign (i.e. European) ships entering Turkish ports were to sail under the French flag, unless they acquired similar grants.

This kind of a concession, granting extraterritorial jurisdiction to consuls and conceding such special privileges as the sultan felt obliged or impelled to offer, is known as a "capitulation," a term which, unfortunately, is misleading in its ambiguity. It is derived not from any idea of surrender of rights, but from the low Latin *caput, capitulum,* "chapter," referring to the sections and articles into which it is divided. The principle of the capitulations was the old one—taken over from antique Mediterranean and Byzantine jurisprudence—that the sovereignty of a state applied only to its subjects. The capitulations granted by the early sultans were not permanent, lasting only, according to Turkish theory, during the life-time of the sultan granting them. Consequently they were continually modified when reaffirmed and subject to abrogation as being only in the nature of a truce with the infidel. The reaffirmations of the capitulations, however, lent more of a continuity to the régime of the capitulations than might at first appear. For instance, the capitulation of Francis I in 1535 drew largely from the concession granted the French in Egypt in 1528, after its capture by the Turks, and this, in turn, is partly traceable to the treaty made by the Sultan of Egypt with St. Louis in 1251. Finally, the great French capitulation of 1740 was made permanently binding; and on it rest all claims of the French and (by extension) of the other foreigners in Turkey up to 1914.[2]

The French capitulation of 1535 became something of a model to be copied in subsequent treaties with other European states. The first capitulation with England was arranged in 1579. Those with the Netherlands followed in 1598 and in 1612. The first capitulation with the German (Holy Roman or Habsburg) Empire was the treaty of 1718, though its merchants had been given conditional privileges in 1616. By the close of the eighteenth century all the Christian countries of Europe, except Switzerland and the States of the Church, had gained recognition for the rights of their citizens engaged in business with Ottoman territories.

It is unnecessary here, however, to enumerate the series of capitulations. For *none of these treaties with western European states granted freedom of navigation in the Black Sea.* The Dardanelles were opened, permitting the ships of

[2] Cf. Pelissie du Raussas, *Le régime des capitulations dans l'Empire Ottoman.* The best collection is that in G. Noradounghian's *Recueil d'actes internationaux de l'Empire Ottoman* (4 Vols. 1897–1903). There is an English translation of important treaties, 1535–1878, in a Parliamentary paper (C. 1953) in *Accounts and Papers,* Vol. 83 of 1878.

the nations to reach Constantinople, upon complying with Turkish formalities at Gallipoli and in port. So in the very first capitulation, that of 1535, we read: "Any ship of the subjects of the king . . . shall be allowed to go where it pleases; and, coming to Constantinople, when it is ready to leave, having taken and paid the *hendjet* (cost of making out the papers) and the *emine* (export tax) and having been searched and visited by the *emin*, is not to be visited in any place, except it be at the castle of the Strait of Gallipoli, without paying more there, or anywhere else, for the right to leave." But the Bosphorus remained closed. At first reading, the text of some capitulations is not clear on this point. The grants of freedom of trade are made in general terms and the Black Sea is not specifically excepted. But the presumption was that it was not included.

An exception was apparently made of Venice for a while, until the Turks were in a position to deal with the first maritime power of the age. Thus (to quote the summary by Young), "by special clauses in the treaties of 1454 and 1479 and by the Capitulations of 1482 and 1513, the Turks granted the Venetians the privilege of trading in the Black Sea, prior to the creation of an Ottoman marine. But this régime always had a provisional character, and with the decline of Venetian shipping and the development of that of the Ottoman Empire, it was replaced by an absolute closure of the Euxine to foreign ships." [8]

COMMERCIAL HISTORY UNDER THE TURK

The commercial history of the Black Sea for the next century is quite obscure. Somehow or other adventurous

[8] Young, *Corps de Droit Ottoman*, Vol. III, p. 66, note.

merchants of Europe found their way to the forbidden shores, apparently chartering Turkish shipping, if not, indeed, finding a way to evade the restrictions which sought to make of the Euxine commerce a Turkish monopoly. These conditions are reflected somewhat dimly in treaties with the English and the Dutch in the seventeenth century.

The English secured a rather obscurely phrased concession in the treaty with the Turks of 1606,[4] which was repeated in the general Capitulation of 1675. It reads as follows: "English merchants and anyone else sailing under the English flag can buy and sell without restriction all kinds of merchandise . . . and transport them by land and sea, and also by the Don to Muscovy or Russia, and carry them into our sacred dominions for trade and also take them to Persia and other conquered provinces." The phrase "sailing under the English flag" may be merely a general description and not apply to the use of the flag on the Black Sea. As for that, the following clause (38) of the same treaty indicates that the ships used by these English traders in the Black Sea were Turkish ships chartered by the English. "If the vessels chartered for Constantinople are forced by contrary winds to stop at Caffa (in the Crimea) or some other port in the same region . . ." they are to be safe from local extortion, etc.; hence the inference that in clause 36 the reference was to English merchants in Turkish ships.[5]

The grant to the Dutch seems less easy to explain away. Clause 57 of the treaty of 1689 reads: "If a contrary wind should drive their vessels, destined for Constantinople, to

---

[4] There is some uncertainty as to the exact date. Hammer gives it as 1604.

[5] Cf. Mischef, *La Mer Noire et les détroits de Constantinople*, p. 30.

Caffa or any other place on that shore, or if they land voluntarily, they shall not be obliged to unload goods which they do not wish to sell, in order to take them by force. No one shall oppose the passage of their vessels or shipping in these waters." [6] No mention occurs here of the chartering of Turkish ships, and, if such documents could be taken at face value, they would seem to indicate that the Dutch, if not also the English, had obtained the right to penetrate the Bosphorus. *But Turkish monopoly was maintained in the Black Sea.*

The historic fact, however, runs counter to such interpretation. Historians agree in insisting that the exclusion of all foreign shipping from the Black Sea was enforced by the Turk. Even when Austria (i.e. the Habsburg monarchy) forced upon Turkey the crushing peace of Passarowitz (1718), the ancient rule that only Turkish ships should sail the Turkish waters was not surrendered. Merchants of the Holy Roman (or Habsburg) Empire might charter boats at Danube ports and send their goods over the Black Sea, but the boats themselves were to be Turkish.

". . . As it has been agreed that the imperial shipping of the Danube will not enter into the Black Sea, they will go by the said river to Ibrail, Isaktche, Kilia and other ports, where are found open boats (caiques) and ships suitable for the navigation of the Black Sea. They will there unload their goods, place them on the (Turkish) ships which they will charter for that object, and they will have full and entire liberty to transport them to Constantinople, the Crimea, Trebizond, and Sinope and the other ports of the Black Sea where their goods find a market."

[6] Noradounghian, *op. cit.*, Vol. I, p. 181.

Twenty years later, in the Treaty of Belgrade (1739), the privileges of "merchants of the provinces under the Emperor of the Romans," to trade in and through the Ottoman Empire were restated on the same general terms as in the capitulations granted the French, English and Dutch.

As a counterpart to the history of the Holy Roman Empire that of France during this period is also instructive. Although it was largely owing to French services that the Treaty of Belgrade (1739) restored Serbia to Turkey, nevertheless, in the capitulations which France secured as a reward (1740), and which were to become the lasting basis of French claims in the Levant, the French flag was still excluded from the Black Sea.

It was not until Russia finally established itself on the northern shores at the end of the eighteenth century, that Turkey was obliged formally to surrender its policy of exclusion of foreign shipping from the Black Sea. The Bosphorus was forced open from the east instead of the west.

III

THE ARRIVAL OF RUSSIA

PETER I AND CATHERINE II

DURING the seventeenth century, Turkey held its own as one of the Great Powers—perhaps the most powerful, with the doubtful exception of France. At the end of that century, however, it began that process of decline which slowly continued until the birth of a new Turkey after the World War. Attacked along the whole of its northern front, it was obliged to surrender most of the Danube Valley (Hungary and Transylvania) to the Habsburgs, the Ukraine and Podalia to Poland and Azof to Russia. The Treaty of Carlowitz in 1699, in which these losses of Turkey were registered, marks the first distinct step in the dismemberment of the Ottoman Empire.

The Turkish monopoly of the Black Sea was now about to be threatened by two Powers, Austria and Russia. Of these, however, Russia alone had reached the shores and set out at once to overcome the Turkish claims.

In 1699, Peter the Great, with characteristic energy and aggressiveness, sent an embassy to Constantinople, on board a Russian man-of-war, one of the Russian squadron he had built in the taking of Azof. This first Russian battle-ship made an impression at Constantinople; but the Turk was not to be over-awed by it, nor by the aggressive attitude of the Russian envoy, and the demand for freedom of navigation on the Black Sea for Russian ships was emphatically refused. The Turkish Government asserted that no foreign vessel should ever sail "the virgin waters of the Black Sea," and, in the face of the intruder, recalled that this rule had been religiously observed in the past. The negotiations failed; the Turks still maintained that Russian ships should not sail out of the Sea of Azof, and that Russian goods destined for Constantinople should cross the Black Sea in Turkish bottoms.[1] Peter's diplomatic failure was followed by his military defeat in a renewal of the war and ten years later (1710) he was forced to surrender his former conquest on the Black Sea, by the Treaty of Pruth, 1711.[2]

A further barrier against the on-coming Russian was erected by Turkey, seconded by France, in the Treaty of Belgrade, 1739. This provided for the destruction of the Russian forts of Azof and forbade Russia to maintain or construct a fleet or other ships in the Sea of Azof or in the Black Sea,[3] and it repeated the rule that all Russian commerce on the Black Sea should be in Turkish ships.[4] This attempt at Russian disarmament, significant in the light of later history, was naturally resented by Russia in proportion as its economic and military development carried it to the shores of the Black Sea.

It was left for Catherine II finally to conquer the Black Sea coastlands for Russia. Although her ambition to divide

[1] Mischef, *op. cit.*, Chapter I. Goriainow, *Le Bosphore et les Dardanelles*, p. 2. The same principle was applied to Austria, by the Treaty of Passarowitz, 1718. See above.

[2] Articles 1 and 2. Dumont, *Corps diplomatique du droit des gens*, Vol. 8, Pt. I, p. 275.

[3] Article 3, Noradounghian, *op. cit.*, Vol. I, p. 258, at 260.

[4] Article 9, *ibid.*, p. 262. France objected to free navigation on the Black Sea, fearing a rival in the Mediterranean, and stimulated Turkish opposition. Cf. Beer, *Orientalische Politik Oesterreichs*, p. 17.

up Turkey, as well as Poland, was not realized, she forced
the Sultan to surrender his control of the north shore of
the Black Sea. To achieve this result, she waged war not
only by land; her fleet was sent around by Gibraltar in
1770 to blockade the Dardanelles and to reach Constantinople from the west—a feat it almost achieved. The enter-
prise failed because of Austria's fears and of Frederick II's
willingness to turn the occasion to his own account by
diverting Catherine to Poland; and also because of Russia's
decision not to make food contraband. Yet, although
Catherine did not win Constantinople, she broke the Turkish policy of exclusion from the Black Sea and, establishing
Russia along its shores, made a new international situation.
For the Black Sea was no longer a Turkish lake.

The Treaty of Kutchuk-Kainardji, 1774, which marked
this first great milestone in Russia's progress, was, therefore,
more than the signal of the Russian arrival. In ending the
exclusively Turkish régime of the Straits and the Black Sea,
it brought the modern phase of the Eastern question; for
other powers besides Russia were destined soon to profit.[5]
Moreover it occupies a unique position in Russo-Turkish
relations. For, as has been frequently pointed out, it in-
augurated the whole series or system of treaties by which
Russia was to assert her claims. All previous treaties between Turkey and Russia were expressly cancelled by it
and all subsequent ones, down to the Crimean War, were
based upon it.[6]

[5] See below, concerning the treaties of 1783, 1784.
[6] Holland, *The Treaty Relations of Russia and Turkey*, p. 2. "The
other great names of the series—Jassy, Bucharest, Ackerman and
Adrianople—one and all have this characteristic in common; the Treaty
of Kutchuk-Kainardji is the text, upon which they are but com-
mentaries." See also *ibid.*, p. 35, for tabular comparison of the relation
of these treaties to each other, clause by clause.

Although Russia's territorial gains on the Black Sea were not large, since the Tartars were merely to be freed from the Turks and made independent—still the foothold had been won from which her conquests could be increased. In the same way a limited recognition of her rights to protect her co-religionists could later be made the excuse for an interference in Turkish affairs which challenged other powers and led to the Crimean War. But the clause which is of chief interest here is that which opened the Black Sea and the Straits to merchant ships flying the Russian flag in time of peace. Russian merchants were to be given the same privileges in Turkish ports and waters as "the most favored nations"—England and France.

The text of Article XI, in which the concession is made, runs as follows: "For the convenience and advantage of the two empires there shall be a free and unimpeded navigation for the merchant ships belonging to the two Contracting Powers, in all the seas which wash their shores; the Sublime Porte grants to Russian merchant vessels, namely, such as are universally employed by the other powers for commerce and in the ports,[7] a free passage from the Black Sea into the White Sea and reciprocally from the White Sea into the Black Sea, as also the power of entering all the ports and harbors situated either on the sea coast, or in the passages and channels which join the seas. . . ."[8]

[7] The Russian text is clearer on this point: ". . . those vessels only which are exactly like the vessels which the other powers employ in the commerce they have with the ports of the Sublime Porte," etc. Mischef, *op. cit.*, p. 185, note.

[8] Text as in Holland, *op. cit.*, p. 42. The original text was in Turkish, Russian and Italian. The Italian text with French translations made "by authority" in Russia is given in Martens, *Recueil* (1st ed.), Vol. I, p. 507, Vol. IV, p. 606, and (2nd ed.) Vol. II, p. 286. The French text is in Noradounghian, *op. cit.*, Vol. I, p. 324, and copied by Mischef, *op. cit.*, p. 184.

The text leaves some obscurity as to the extent of the grant, for the term "White Sea" (bahr-i-sefid) was applied to the Sea of Marmora as well as to the Mediterranean.[9] In 1779 a *convention explicative* was added to the treaty, insisting (Article VI) upon the limitation of Russian ships passing the Straits to those permitted England and France in their capitulations.[10] Finally, in 1783, a sweeping commercial treaty, much resembling the capitulations granted other countries, elaborated in some eighty-one clauses the conditions under which the Russian commercial flag was to be permitted, like that of England and France, the entry into Turkish ports. Russian commercial ships were to be permitted to pass the Straits without payment of any customs dues.

Catherine's ambition, however, was political rather than commercial. It was aimed at nothing less than the conquest of Constantinople itself. With Austria as an ally she waged a new war on Turkey in 1789. But England, Holland and Prussia intervened (France was pre-occupied with the Revolution) and prevented the dismemberment of Turkey.[11] Poland became the victim instead. Russia, although victorious over the Turks, surrendered its conquests west of the Dniester, by the Treaty of Jassy, 1792. The Treaty

[9] Young, *op. cit.*, Vol. III, p. 67, note.

[10] Martens, *op. cit.* (2nd ed.), Vol. I, p. 658. The reference is blind, although it is repeated in 1783, for there are no prescriptions as to form and size of ship in the capitulations of France and England. Young, *op. cit.*, Vol. III, p. 68, note.

[11] Treaties of Sistova (Turkey and Austria) in 1791, and of Jassy (Turkey and Russia) 1792. The text of Sistova is in Noradounghian, *op. cit.*, Vol. II, p. 13; L. Neumann, *Recueil des traités et conventions conclus par l'Autriche*, etc., Vol. I, p. 463; Martens, *Recueil* (2nd ed.), Vol. V, p. 245; that of Jassy is in Noradounghian, *op. cit.*, Vol. II, p. 16; Martens, *Recueil* (1st ed.), Vol. V, p. 53, (2nd ed.) Vol. V, p. 291 (German translation); Martens and Cussey, *Recueil annuel*, etc., Vol. II, p. 65.

of Kainardji was again confirmed, along with the *convention explicative* and the commercial treaty of 1783, "since commerce is the truest and most constant bond of reciprocal harmony." [12]

As Russian merchant ships entered the Straits from the Black Sea end, it was obvious that the old principle governing the use of the Straits was broken. The other nations therefore sought to obtain the new advantages. Austria gained free passage for her ships of commerce in 1784.[13] England was not admitted to the full benefits of this régime till 1799, when the privilege was granted by an official note from the Porte, which was reaffirmed in 1802.[14] France received the concession in 1802, Prussia in 1806.[15]

THE NAPOLEONIC ERA

The arrival of Russia had made the question of the Straits one of general European policy, but so far the solution affected the commercial rather than the naval side of the problem. The Turkish commercial monopoly was broken, but its right to control and so prohibit the passage

[12] Art. VIII.

[13] Noradounghian, *op. cit.*, Vol. I, pp. 379–382. Sanad of February, 1784. See also firman of May, 1784, in Martens, *Nouveau Recueil Général*, Vol. 15, p. 462: "Since the merchant ships of the German court, friend and neighbour of the Sublime Porte, since the peace of Belgrade, have carried on commerce on the White Sea without being permitted to navigate the Black Sea, that court has requested the Sultan to permit them to sail out of the rivers into the Black Sea *and from that sea into the White Sea,* and so back and forth. The Sultan permits German merchants to freely carry on their business on land, sea and rivers and has given a sanad to the Austrian Minister." It is clearly stated here that the request was for the right to navigate not only the Black Sea but also the Straits.

[14] Hertslet, *Commercial Treaties*, Vol. V, p. 499, Vol. VII, p. 1021.

[15] *Ibid.*, p. 78.

of foreign war-ships through its territorial waters remained unimpaired. The problem of naval strategy was still to be settled; indeed it was hardly a problem, except for Russia, prior to the nineteenth century.

Napoleon's Egyptian expedition definitely opened the modern phase of the Near Eastern question as we know it. France, for centuries the one Christian power most friendly to Turkey, now became an invader. England had its attention drawn to the strategic importance of the Near Eastern route to India, and, for the first time awake to its importance, began to play in earnest that rôle in the Levant which it has followed with relative consistency until the present war—that of supporter of the Ottoman. Russia, drawn to the Straits through the same Napoleonic invasion, became the main competitor of England for the control of those who controlled the Straits, since Constantinople stands at the cross-roads of the route to India. and the route to Odessa. Hence, as the Napoleonic wars revealed increasing signs of the weakness of the Ottoman Empire, the three-fold contest (for Austria was not so directly involved) of England, France and Russia centered to a large degree at Constantinople.

The first effect of Napoleon's campaign in the Orient was to throw Turkey—so far as the Straits were concerned —into the hands of Russia. The appeal of the Sultan to the Czar brought a Russian fleet, which entered the Bosphorus in September, 1798; and the resulting alliance [16] between Turkey and Russia was joined a few days later by England.[17] The barriers once down, the Russian fleet passed

[16] Treaty of Constantinople, December 23, 1798; cf. Noradounghian, *op. cit.*, Vol. II, p. 24.

[17] January 5, 1799, *ibid.*, p. 28.

and repassed the Straits without regard to treaty stipulations, and Russia began definitely to formulate plans for the partition of Turkey (1800).[18] A year later Napoleon, victorious at Marengo, with western Europe breaking up at his behest, was planning anew the march on India, this time with the half-crazed Paul I as his ally. As a counter to the danger which lurked behind the Straits, England took Malta and secured Egypt by an Indian army. The murder of the Czar (March, 1801) and the accession of Alexander I, friendly to England, made possible the peace of Amiens (March, 1802).[19]

The initial policy of Alexander was to preserve, rather than destroy, a weak Ottoman power at the Straits, and to turn its weakness to Russia's advantage.[20] The Russian fleet continued to pass the Straits, for, in the renewed war with Napoleon, Russia was again England's ally; and when Turkey, won over by Napoleon's ambassador Sebastiani, declared war on the side of France, Britain came to the support of Russia, sending a fleet which forced the Dardanelles and actually reached, and for a moment overawed, Constantinople (March, 1807). The energy of Sebastiani in hastily organizing the defense of the city caused its withdrawal, however, without having achieved its purpose. Four months later (July 7, 1807) the Treaty of Tilsit gave a new turn to events.[21]

---

[18] Dascovici, *La question du Bosphore et des Dardanelles*, pp. 147–148.

[19] For the section relating to Turkey cf. Noradounghian, *op. cit.*, Vol. II, p. 50. A separate commercial treaty was concluded a month later which, for the first time, allowed the commercial freedom of the Black Sea and the Straits, by extending the Capitulation of 1740 to include this grant; cf. Noradounghian, *op. cit.*, Vol. II, pp. 51–53.

[20] Cf. Dascovici, *op. cit.*, p. 150.

[21] Driault, *La question d'Orient en 1807*, in *Revue d'histoire diplomatique*, Vol. XIV (1900), p. 436, states that after the Treaty of Tilsit

It is not necessary here to enter into the details of Napoleon's and Alexander's scheme for the partition of the Orient; but it should be recalled that the main point in that grandiose plan upon which the two emperors failed to reach agreement was the problem of who should hold Constantinople and the Straits.[22] More important, however, than these arrangements, because more lasting in its influence upon the history of the Straits, was the fact that England, now again obliged to be friendly to Turkey, made with the Porte the Treaty of Constantinople, commonly known as the Peace of the Dardanelles, which contained the first formal assertion, in international treaty, of the principle of the closing of the straits to ships of war in time of peace.[23]

It was significant that this first statement should refer to the regulation as the "ancient rule of the Ottoman Empire" which excluded war-ships of every nation from entering either the Dardanelles or Bosphorus. Article II of the treaty runs as follows:

"As it has at all times been forbidden for vessels of war to enter into the canal of Constantinople, that is, into the Straits of the Dardanelles and into that of the Black Sea, and as that

---

the Czar instructed the Russian war-ships in the Mediterranean to pass into the Black Sea, *if the Porte gives them permission;* otherwise they are to go through the Straits of Gibraltar to French ports for shelter and supplies. Thus Russia recognized the rule.

[22] For the tortuous negotiations see Tatistcheff, *Alexandre Ier et Napoleon d'après leur correspondance inédite,* 1801–1812 (Paris, 1891); Cf. Phillipson and Buxton, *The Question of the Bosphorus and the Dardanelles,* pp. 41, 42.

[23] For the story of negotiations see the two-volume account of the British Ambassador, Sir Robert Adair, *The Negotiations for the Peace of the Dardanelles in 1808–9* (London, 1845). The text is in Noradounghian, *op. cit.,* Vol. II, p. 81.

ancient rule of the Ottoman Empire should be observed henceforth in times of peace with reference to any Powers whatsoever, the Court of Britain promises also to conform to this principle."

The clause was cleverly drawn. Turkey insists on her sovereign rights and wins from Britain a formal recognition of them. In reality, Britain becomes the guardian of the Straits almost as much as Turkey. The provision constitutes the germ of the international convention laid down in the Straits Convention of 1841 when England again was to have its say as to the settlement of the question.[24]

Upon the whole, the Napoleonic period left the matter as Turkey and England wished.

RUSSIAN TRIUMPHS

At the Congress of Vienna the question of the Straits was not considered, nor even the larger problem of the Ottoman Empire. The British Government supported Metternich's plan to guarantee the existence of Turkey, but the Porte itself was suspicious of too much guardianship by the British. British mediation suggested too nearly the idea of a protectorate. In a sense, therefore, Turkey played into the hands of the Czar, who wished to avoid any guarantee of Ottoman integrity; and Turkey remained outside the European state-system.

But the Near Eastern question could not be shelved. European Turkey in the years following the Congress of Vienna became the theater of feud and massacre, culminating in the horrors of the Greek War of Independence

[24] Cf. Phillipson and Buxton, *op. cit.*, p. 43. Goriainow, *op. cit.*, Chap. II, gives Russian data.

(1821–1829). Official England temporized with its "ancient ally" the Turk, and played with Metternich upon the pacific temper of Alexander I. But when the forceful Nicholas I took control of Russia (1825), he quickly cowed the Porte into accepting the terms of the Treaty of Ackerman (October, 1826), which, among its other terms, granted Russia complete freedom "in all the seas and waters of the Ottoman Empire without any exception" for its merchant shipping.[25]

Meanwhile Britain brought about an accord with France and Russia for joint intervention in the Eastern question,[26] but that British reluctance to weaken the Ottoman power, which muddled British policy with reference to Greece, finally left it to the Czar to exert the coercion necessary for securing a settlement. Russian armies marched across the Balkans for the first time and forced upon the Turk the humiliating terms of the Treaty of Adrianople (September, 1829).

"In the long history of the Eastern Question, the Treaty of Adrianople is inferior only in importance to those of Kainardji and Berlin." [27] The independence of Greece not only marked a further stage in the dissolution of the Turkish Empire; it also changed the standing of Turkish shipping, since so many of the maritime interests of the Ottoman Empire were in Greek hands. But the treaty as well (Article VII) reiterated in most sweeping terms the grant of

[25] Article VII, clause 2. Cf. Noradounghian, *op. cit.*, Vol. II, p. 120; *British and Foreign State Papers*, Vol. 13, p. 899; Martens, *Nouveau Recueil*, Vol. VI, p. 1053.
[26] Treaty of London. The protocols are in Martens, *Nouveau Recueil*, Vol. XII, pp. 1–265; treaty, *ibid.*, p. 465; Noradounghian, *op. cit.*, Vol. II, p. 130.
[27] Marriott, *The Eastern Question*, p. 199.

freedom to Russian commercial ships in all Ottoman waters, with the additional and unique proviso that no visit or search was to be exercised over Russian vessels passing the Straits. The degree of Russian domination was expressed in the additional provision that any act or interference by the Turk to this complete freedom would be met by "reprisals against the Ottoman Empire."

The text of Article VII of the treaty runs as follows:

"Russian subjects shall enjoy, throughout the whole extent of the Ottoman Empire, as well by land as by sea, the full and entire freedom of trade secured to them by the treaties concluded heretofore between the two High Contracting Powers. This freedom of trade shall not be molested in any way, nor shall it be fettered in any case, or under any pretext, by any prohibition or restriction whatsoever, nor in consequence of any regulation or measure, whether of public government or internal legislation. Russian subjects, ships and merchandise shall be protected from all violence and imposition. The first shall remain under the exclusive jurisdiction and control of the Russian minister and consuls; Russian ships shall never be subjected to any search on the part of the Ottoman authorities, neither out at sea nor in any of the ports or roadsteads under the dominion of the Sublime Porte; and all merchandise or goods belonging to a Russian subject may, after payment of the custom-house dues imposed by the tariffs, be freely sold, deposited on land in the warehouses of the owner or consignee, or transshipped on board another vessel of any nation whatsoever, without the Russian subject being required, in this case, to give notice of the same to any of the local authorities, and much less to ask their permission so to do. It is expressly agreed that the different kinds of wheat coming from Russia shall partake of the same privileges, and that their free transit shall never, under any pretext, suffer the least difficulty or hindrance.

"The Sublime Porte engages, moreover, to take especial care that the trade and navigation of the Black Sea, particularly, shall be impeded in no manner whatsoever. For this purpose it admits and declares the passage of the Strait of Constantinople and that of the Dardanelles to be entirely free and open to Russian vessels under the merchant flag, laden or in ballast, whether they come from the Black Sea for the purpose of entering the Mediterranean, or whether, coming from the Mediterranean, they wish to enter the Black Sea; such vessels, provided they be merchant ships, whatever their size and tonnage, shall be exposed to no hindrance or annoyance of any kind, as above provided. The two Courts shall agree upon the most fitting means for preventing all delay in issuing the necessary instructions. In virtue of the same principle the passage of the Strait of Constantinople and that of the Dardanelles is declared free and open to all the merchant ships of Powers who are at peace with the Sublime Porte, whether going into the Russian ports of the Black Sea or coming from them, laden or in ballast, upon the same conditions which are stipulated for vessels under the Russian flag.

"Lastly, the Sublime Porte, recognizing in the Imperial Court of Russia the right of securing the necessary guarantees for this full freedom of trade and navigation in the Black Sea, declares solemnly, that on its part not the least obstacle shall ever, under any pretext whatsoever, be opposed to it. Above all, it promises never to allow itself henceforth to stop or detain vessels laden or in ballast, whether Russian or belonging to nations with whom the Ottoman Porte shall not be in a state of declared war, which vessels shall be passing through the Strait of Constantinople and that of the Dardanelles, on their way from the Black Sea into the Mediterranean, or from the Mediterranean into the Russian ports of the Black Sea. And if, which God forbid, any one of the stipulations contained in the present article should be infringed, and the remonstrances of the Russian minister thereupon should fail in obtaining a

full and prompt redress, the Sublime Porte recognizes before-
hand in the Imperial Court of Russia the right of considering
such an infraction as an act of hostility, and of immediately
having recourse to reprisals against the Ottoman Empire." [28]

In 1832, the existence of the Ottoman Empire was threatened by the great revolt of Mehemet Ali, whose troops,
overrunning most of Asiatic Turkey, were threatening the
Straits. Again, as in the Napoleonic crisis, Russia profited.
France was on the side of Mehemet, England declined to
act; and the hard-pressed Sultan was obliged to invite Russia to come in, with fleet and army, and save him from the
rebels. The results were a Russian fleet and troops for the
defense of Constantinople itself, the passage of the Dardanelles by Russian warships, and the establishment of what
amounted to a Russian protectorate over Turkey.

The treaty which embodied these conditions was signed
at Unkiar-Skelessi in 1833. [29] By it Russia guaranteed the
existence of Turkey, offering the use of Russian arms to
maintain it. The Sultan's *quid pro quo* was indicated in a
separate, secret clause:

"His Majesty, the Emperor of all the Russias, wishing to
spare the Sublime Ottoman Porte the expense and inconvenience
which might be occasioned by affording substantial aid, will
not ask for that aid if circumstances should place the Sublime
Porte under the obligation of furnishing it. The Sublime
Ottoman Porte, in place of the help which it is bound to
furnish in case of need, according to the principle of reci-

[28] This is a most unusual clause, and indicates the extent of Turkey's
helplessness.
For a discussion of the treaty see Phillipson and Buxton, *op. cit.*,
p. 53. Text in Noradounghian, *op. cit.*, Vol. II, p. 166; Martens, *Nouveau
Recueil*, Vol. VII, p. 143.
[29] Noradounghian, *op. cit.*, Vol. II, p. 230. It was to run for eight years.
Phillipson and Buxton, *op. cit.*, p. 62.

procity in the open treaty, shall limit its action in favor of
the Imperial Court of Russia to closing the Straits of the
Dardanelles, that is to say, not to permit any foreign ship of
war to enter therein under any pretext whatever." [30]

The Treaty of Unkiar-Skelessi marks the zenith of Russian influence at Constantinople, and the secret clause is
the expression of it. While its ambiguity has been the subject of much discussion, it was taken by Russia at least to
mean that it guaranteed a free passage for Russian warships
through the Straits "in case of need"—which covers every
pretext—and closed the entrance to the Black Sea to every
other power. [31]

Palmerston objected that these terms were inconsistent
with the treaty of 1809, by which the Porte had agreed to
prohibit the passage to ships of war of *any* foreign power.
The English fleet sailed up to Besika Bay and France sent
an identic note to that of England. But no one wanted war,
and the western Powers waited their chance.

The United States, strangely enough, was to test the
strength of the Russian influence in 1835. An American
frigate reached Constantinople and tried to secure permission to pass to the Black Sea. The Porte submitted the request to Boutenieff, the Russian Ambassador, who advised
that it be refused, for fear the European Powers use the
incident as a pretext for their own ships to pass. [32]

[30] *Ibid.*, p. 231.
[31] Cf. Marriott, *op. cit.*, p. 210. See discussion in Phillipson and Buxton,
op. cit., pp. 61–67.
[32] Phillipson and Buxton, *op. cit.*, p. 69.

IV

FROM THE TREATY OF LONDON (1840) TO THE CONVENTION OF THE STRAITS (1841)

THE secret clause of the Treaty of Unkiar-Skelessi was soon whispered abroad in rival chancelleries, and European diplomacy reflected the disturbance it created. While England and France protested, Metternich's deft hand secured from Russia an avowal of innocent purposes,[1] which tided Europe through the crisis. The insincerity of Turkey toward Russia, which had imposed such humiliating terms upon it, also made Russia's triumph less secure and therefore less menacing. It was obvious as well that England and France would not leave to Russia the enjoyment of the Treaty of Unkiar-Skelessi if they could help it.

In 1839 war broke out again between the Sultan and Mehemet Ali, resulting in the complete defeat of the Turk. Again the Ottoman Empire seemed about to dissolve, with Russia waiting to share the spoils on the north and France about to profit in Egypt by its friendship for Mehemet Ali. England had no desire to see either of these results. Metternich had, at the outbreak of the war, proposed action by the European Concert, and France and England quickly

---

[1] Convention of Münchengrätz, 1833. Both parties to combine to maintain the Turkish Empire as against others designing its overthrow, etc. Martens, *Recueil des traités et conventions conclus par la Russie* (1898), Vol. IV, pt. I, pp. 445ff.; Mischef, *op. cit.*, pp. 293ff.

took up the idea of common action, although French public opinion objected to too close association with English aims. Russia, taking advantage of this rift between England and France, refused to join and advised the Sultan to make peace with Mehemet directly, without reference to Europe. Russia felt that the action of the Powers, if they came together, would undo the advantages she had held since Unkiar-Skelessi. However, Metternich acted quickly and anticipated objections by having the Austrian ambassador at Constantinople present the Sultan a *collective note* from the Five Powers, stating that these Powers had reached an accord on the Eastern question, and holding the Porte to "abstain from any final decision without their concurrence and to await the results of their interest in its welfare." [2]

Russia having apparently given in on the formal question of the acceptance of the Concert, the Czar's ambassador at London made the most of the situation to sow dissension between France and England. The Czar's strong personal dislike of France was an element in the situation, playing into the plans of Palmerston, whose objections to the French plan of favoring Mehemet Ali's ambitions upon Syria were soon shared by Berlin and Vienna as well as St. Petersburg. Then Russia opened new diplomatic possibilities. To Palmerston's surprise, the Government of the Czar went so far as to intimate a willingness to reconsider the Treaty of Unkiar-Skelessi, stating that the Czar had regarded that treaty not as an implement for establishing an absolute protectorate over Turkey but merely as a means of safety for the Porte. [3] The Treaty of Unkiar-Skelessi

[2] *British and Foreign State Papers*, Vol. 28, p. 408.
[3] Goriainow, *op. cit.*, p. 67.

might be revised by proclaiming the closing of the Straits *at all times* a universally recognized principle of the public law of Europe. Upon the bases of such plans the Czar's Government then proposed that England's fleet attack Mehemet's port of Alexandria and the Russian army come down to Constantinople to safeguard the capital from the Syrian rebels. Palmerston naturally refused to enter upon a plan which brought the Russians to Constantinople alone, and it was only after rather protracted negotiations, to which France was not a party—her interest in Egypt having led to independent negotiations with Turkey—that an agreement was reached by the four Powers of Russia, Britain, Prussia and Austria.

The Treaty of London, in which this agreement was registered, began by stating (Article I) that the Contracting Powers had come to an agreement with Turkey as to what terms Mehemet Ali should receive, and that (Article II) in case Mehemet refused to accept them, they, the Powers, would undertake to force him to do so. "Their Majesties engage to take, at the request of the Sultan, measures concerted and settled between them, in order to carry that arrangement into effect." Article III states that if Constantinople is threatened by invasion the Powers will send help, and Article IV safeguards the Sultan's sovereignty for the future, in case Russia and the western Powers should—for this one time—send their armed forces through the Straits.

These two articles are fundamental in the history of the international law of the Straits. They run as follows:

"Article III. If Mehemet Ali, after having refused to submit to the conditions of the arrangement above-mentioned (specified in a separate Act), should direct his land or sea forces against Constantinople, the High Contracting Parties, upon the express demand of the Sultan, addressed to their Representatives at Constantinople, agree, in such case, to comply with the request of that Sovereign, and to provide for the defense of his throne by means of a cooperation agreed upon by mutual consent, for the purpose of placing the two Straits of the Bosphorus and Dardanelles, as well as the capital of the Ottoman Empire, in security against all aggression.

"It is further agreed that the forces which, in virtue of such concert, may be sent as aforesaid, shall there remain so employed as long as their presence shall be required by the Sultan; and when His Highness shall deem their presence no longer necessary, the said forces shall simultaneously withdraw, and shall return to the Black Sea and to the Mediterranean respectively.

"Article IV. It is, however, expressly understood, that the cooperation mentioned in the preceding Article, and destined to place the Straits of the Dardanelles and of the Bosphorus, and the Ottoman capital, under the temporary safeguard of the High Contracting Parties against all aggression of Mehemet Ali, shall be considered only as a measure of exception adopted at the express demand of the Sultan, and solely for his defense in the single case above-mentioned; but *it is agreed that such measure shall not derogate in any degree from the ancient rule of the Ottoman Empire, in virtue of which it has in all times been prohibited for ships of war of foreign Powers to enter the Straits of the Dardanelles and of the Bosphorus.* And the Sultan, on the one hand, hereby declares that, excepting the contingency above-mentioned, it is his firm resolution to maintain in future this principle invariably established as the ancient rule of his Empire; and as long as the Porte is at peace, to admit no foreign ship of war into the Straits of the Bosphorus and of the Dardanelles; on the other hand, their Majesties the Queen of the United Kingdom of Great Britain and Ireland, the Emperor of Austria, King of Hungary and Bohemia, the King of Prussia, and the Emperor of all the Russias, engage to respect this determination of the Sultan, and to conform to the above-mentioned principle." [4]

The significance of the Treaty of London is that it translates into European public law a principle which had previously been recognized only in the dealings of individual Powers with Turkey. The "ancient rule of the Ottoman Empire" was formulated by the Sultan for his dealings with the various States. Now "four of the leading Powers jointly recognized in a formal international instrument the applicability of the rule of closing the Bosphorus and the Dardanelles to warships of all States, whilst the Sultan, engaging to observe this rule in general, formally surrendered his former right of opening the Straits at discretion." [5]

The next year France joined in a general treaty along these lines, recognizing the obligation of the Sultan to close the Straits to foreign ships of war in time of peace. The Convention was accepted by other Powers later, and became a general rule of European international law.[6]

The text of this Convention, to which discussion naturally reverts, is very brief and clear, consisting of the fol-

[4] Hertslet, *Map of Europe*, Vol. II, p. 1008. French text in *British and Foreign State Papers*, Vol. 28, p. 342, and Noradounghian, *op. cit.*, Vol. II, p. 303ff. *Parliamentary Papers*, Vol. 83 (1878), No. 43, p. 20.

[5] Phillipson and Buxton, *op. cit.*, p. 77. By a further protocol the Porte "reserves to itself as heretofore to deliver Passes to light vessels under flag of War which may be employed according to custom for the service of the correspondence of the legations of friendly Powers." Hertslet, *op. cit.*, Vol. II, p. 1021. This was incorporated in the Convention of 1841.

[6] *Ibid.*, p. 79. The detailed story of the diplomacy of 1840–41 is given in Mischef, *op. cit.*, Chapter V, and in Goriainow, *op. cit.*, Chapter X. A good summary is given by Dascovici, *op. cit.*, p. 184ff.

lowing three articles and an additional one dealing with ratifications:

"Article I. His Highness the Sultan, on the one part, declares that he is firmly resolved to maintain for the future the principle invariably established as the ancient rule of the Empire, and in virtue of which it has at all times been prohibited for the Ships of War of Foreign Powers to enter the Straits of the Dardanelles and the Bosphorus; and that so long as the Porte is at peace, His Highness will admit no Foreign Ship of War into the said Straits.

"And their Majesties the Queen of the United Kingdom of Great Britain and Ireland, the Emperor of Austria, King of Hungary and Bohemia, the King of the French, the King of Prussia, and the Emperor of all the Russias, on the other part, engage to respect this determination of the Sultan and to conform themselves to the principle above declared.

"Article II. It is understood that in recording the inviolability of the ancient rule of the Ottoman Empire mentioned in the preceding Article, the Sultan reserves to himself, as in past times, to deliver Firmans of passage for light Vessels under Flag of War, which shall be employed as is usual in the service of the Missions of Foreign Powers.

"Article III. His Highness, the Sultan, reserves to himself to communicate the present Convention to all the Powers with whom the Sublime Porte is in relations of friendship, inviting them to accede thereto."

This Convention, reaffirmed in its essentials in the Treaty of Paris in 1856, and again in the Conference of London in 1871, was the fundamental document in the international law of the Straits down to the war of 1914. The significant phrase is short and clear: "So long as the Porte is at peace, His Highness will admit no Foreign Ships of War into the said Straits."

V

THE TREATY OF PARIS, 1856

THE Straits Convention, which had robbed Russia of its predominance in Turkish affairs, could not be accepted by Russia with good grace. Nicholas began to make significant reference to the "sick man of Europe" whose inheritance should be divided among the Powers.[1] The first step toward this end, however, showed that the inheritors could not agree. The quarrel over the spoils began, not over the control of the Straits, but over prerogatives of Holy Russia as protector of the Orthodox clergy and of France as the ancient champion of Catholicism in the Orient, at the holy places in the Sultan's realm. Russia finally, unable to secure full privileges from the Porte, took matters into her own hands and invaded Turkey in 1853.[2]

The action of Russia at once involved France, as Napoleon III was strongly committed to a clerical policy, and England, following its traditional lines, was drawn into common action with France in order to defend the integrity of the Ottoman Empire. The British and French fleets

[1] It was not a new expression. See Palmerston in the House of Commons, July 11, 1833. For the proposed partition scheme see *Parliamentary Papers*, Vol. 71 (1844), pt. V, I. Cf. Martens, *Traités conclus par la Russie*, Vol. XII, p. 306ff. (Phillipson and Buxton, *op. cit.*, p. 84.)

[2] Nesselrode, the Russian minister, stated that they came not to make war but simply to secure material guarantees. It was Turkey that finally took the offensive and tried to drive the Russians from the soil of Turkey.

were despatched into the Sea of Marmora, technically justifying themselves by the Straits Convention. Russia claimed that, under pretext of saving Turkey, they had openly violated the Convention. The situation rapidly drifted into war, France and England declaring war on Russia after making a treaty of alliance with Turkey. The war was fought out on the Crimea, by the aid of the allied fleets which struck at the great Russian fortress on the Black Sea, Sebastopol.

In the peace negotiations, which were begun before the Crimean War was finished, the most difficult questions to settle were the questions of the Straits and the Black Sea. It was to be expected that, after a disastrous war, Russia would surrender the position it had held, with reference to Turkey, but to accept the full humiliation of a neutralized sea on its southern frontier was to accept the terms of the vanquished. This it found itself obliged to do after the fall of Sebastopol.

The Treaty of Paris, in which these important clauses were embodied, was the result of the Conference at Paris of the Powers of Europe (including Sardinia) and for the next fourteen years it determined the status of the Straits.[8]

According to Article VII, Turkey was "admitted to participate in the advantages of the public law and system of Europe." Apart from the territorial settlements, the Treaty dealt mainly with three points: the question of the Straits;

[8] Text in Hertslet, *Map of Europe*, Vol. II, p. 1250; Phillipson, *Termination of War and Treaties of Peace*, pp. 350-7; Holland, *European Concert in the Eastern Question*, pp. 241ff. For full discussion of the Conference of Paris see Goriainow, Mischef, Dascovici, *op. cit.* and in Debidour, *Histoire diplomatique de l'Europe* (Paris, 1891), etc. As the treaty dealt but slightly with the Straits, Phillipson and Buxton have rather slight treatment.

the neutralization of the Black Sea; and the navigation of the Danube.

With reference to the Straits, a separate Convention between the six Powers (including Sardinia) and the Sultan, signed the same time as the Treaty and attached to it (by Article X of the Treaty), reaffirmed textually the clauses of the Convention of the Straits. A further clause was added (Article XIX), in view of the proposals in the Treaty itself for the control of the navigation of the Danube, by which each of the Powers was permitted to send through the Straits two light vessels of war for service off the mouth of the Danube. Otherwise the Convention which regulated the régime of the Straits in 1856 merely reenacted the Convention of 1841.

The most significant act of the Conference at Paris, however, was the declaration of the neutralization of the Black Sea, an attempt to forestall future complications in the Near East by imposing a sufficiently sweeping prohibition on Russian preparedness. Russia was to be denied not merely a fleet on its southern coastal waters but even arsenals along its shores. The clauses of the Treaty run as follows:

"Article XI. The Black Sea is neutralized; its Waters and its Ports, thrown open to the Mercantile Marine of every Nation, are formally and perpetually interdicted to the Flag of War, either of the Powers possessing its Coasts, or of any other Power, with the exceptions mentioned in Articles XIV and XIX of the present Treaty.

"Article XII. Free from any impediment, the Commerce in the Ports and Waters of the Black Sea shall be subject only to regulations of Health, Customs, and Police, framed in a spirit favorable to the development of Commercial transactions.

"In order to afford to the Commercial and Maritime interests of every Nation the security which is desired, Russia and the Sublime Porte will admit Consuls into their Ports situated upon the Coast of the Black Sea, in conformity with the principles of International Law.

"Article XIII. The Black Sea being neutralized according to the terms of Article XI, the maintenance or establishment upon its Coast of Military-Maritime Arsenals becomes alike unnecessary and purposeless; in consequence, His Majesty the Emperor of All the Russias, and His Imperial Majesty the Sultan, engage not to establish or to maintain upon that Coast any Military-Maritime Arsenal.

"Article XIV. Their Majesties, the Emperor of All the Russias and the Sultan, having concluded a Convention for the purpose of settling the Force and the Number of Light Vessels necessary for the service of their coasts, which they reserve to themselves to maintain in the Black Sea, that Convention is annexed to the present Treaty and shall have the same force and validity as if it formed an integral part thereof. It can not be either annulled or modified without the assent of the Powers signing the present Treaty."

The neutralization of the Black Sea was, in a sense, an innovation in international law, since it attempted to apply to a sea a new conception, that of neutralization, to be added to those of the simple categories of Grotius, free sea and territorial sea (*mare apertum* or *mare liberum* and *mare clausum*).[4] It was an application to the sea of a principle hitherto confined to land. But the proposition was not made in the constructive sense nor applied in a way that gave promise of future development toward the great goal of general naval disarmament. It was a chapter of naval strategy by which the advantages of victory could be

[4] Cf. Phillipson and Buxton, *op. cit.*, p. 99.

maintained against Russia. It lacked the element of internationalization, for just outside the Bosphorus the fleets of Europe could ride unchecked, and in time of war the Sultan might let them through; disarmament was enforced on the Russians alone. The complement of the plan, the neutralization of the Straits, was lacking, for Turkey was still a Power.

VI

THE TREATY OF LONDON, 1871

THE years following the Treaty of Paris were those in which the nationalist spirit of Europe revealed itself in fuller and fuller consciousness as the new railways and steam shipping wrought together the economic fabric of the State, while education and the spread of journalism made possible a citizenship responsive to large political appeals. The era of Italy's and Germany's unification, and of England's world wide development, could not well leave Russia suffering the constant sense of humiliation in the limitation upon her power of defense along the whole southern frontier. But, though the Czar Alexander was deeply stung by the reminder of defeat,[1] he refused steadily to bring up the question of the revision of the Treaty of Paris so long as the proposition was likely to bring another war.[2] His patience was rewarded, however, by the year 1870, when the Franco-Prussian war offered a chance for Russia to recover what she had surrendered, since western Europe was too much preoccupied with its own affairs to interfere.

Bismarck's assent to Russia's denunciation of the objectionable terms of the Treaty of Paris was easily won, and

[1] Goriainow, *op. cit.*, pp. 144ff.
[2] France approached her in 1858 before the war with Austria, and Austria after the war, 1859, and again in 1867. William I of Prussia approached her also after the Seven Weeks' War in 1866. But, although he plainly showed how he felt, Alexander refused to act.

the other Powers not being in a position to make war, Gortchakoff sent a circular dispatch in October, 1870.[3] In it Russia protested that fifteen years' experience had proved the falseness of the assumptions in the Treaty of Paris that neutralization of the Black Sea would safeguard the peace of all interested. In reality, while Russia was disarming in the Black Sea, Turkey maintained unlimited naval forces in the Aegean and Straits, and France and England could mobilize their squadrons in the Mediterranean. There was, so he claimed, a contradiction between the Treaty itself and the attached Convention of the Straits; the former forbade war-ships to sail the Black Sea at any time, the latter prohibited them from passing the Straits into the Black Sea only in time of peace. This exposed the shores of Russia to attack from even less powerful states, while Russia was unprepared. Moreover, in the interval the treaty had been modified with reference to Moldavia and Wallachia; infractions had occurred in that "whole squadrons" of foreign men-of-war had been admitted to the Black Sea, etc.[4]

"After maturely considering this question, His Imperial Majesty has arrived at the following conclusions, which you are instructed to bring to the knowledge of the Government to which you are accredited:

[3] Hertslet, *Map of Europe*, Vol. III, p. 1892; Goriainow, *op. cit.*, p. 156; Phillipson and Buxton, *op. cit.*, p. 105.

[4] "In 1871 a return laid before Parliament showed that the number of Foreign Ships of War which had passed the Straits were: In 1862, 1 British; in 1866, 1 American; in 1868, 1 American, 2 Austrian, 1 French, 1 Russian; in 1869, 1 Prussian. It also appeared that in 7 other instances, questions had arisen with regard to the passage of Foreign Ships of War through the Straits, but that in no case had a violation of treaty been shown to have taken place." Hertslet, *op. cit.*, Vol. III, p. 1895, note. Also Young, *in loco*.

"Our illustrious Master can not admit, *de jure*, that Treaties, violated in several of their essential and general clauses, should remain binding in other clauses directly affecting the interests of his Empire.

"His Imperial Majesty can not admit, *de facto*, that the security of Russia should depend on a fiction which has not stood the test of time, and should be imperilled by her respect for engagements which have not been observed in their integrity.

"Confiding in the feelings of justice of the Powers who have signed the Treaty in 1856, as well as in their consciousness of their own dignity, the Emperor commands you to declare that His Imperial Majesty can not any longer hold himself bound by the stipulations of the Treaty of 18/30th March, 1856, as far as they restrict his Sovereign Rights in the Black Sea;

"That His Imperial Majesty deems himself both entitled and obliged to denounce to His Majesty the Sultan the Special and Additional Convention appended to the said Treaty, which fixes the number and size of the Vessels of War which the two Powers bordering on the Black Sea shall keep in that Sea;

"That His Majesty loyally informs of this the Powers who have signed and guaranteed the General Treaty, of which the Convention in question forms an integral part;

"That His Majesty restores to the Sultan the full exercise of his rights in this respect, resuming the same for himself. . . ." [5]

The note concluded with the statement that the Czar had no desire to revive the Eastern question, and adhered to the general principles of 1856 which fixed the position of Turkey in the European system.[6]

[5] Hertslet, *op. cit.*, Vol. III, pp. 1894-5.

[6] The circular was accompanied by special despatches to each government. See Goriainow, *op. cit.*, p. 162. (Summarized by Phillipson and

England protested at once. Lord Granville, Foreign Secretary, refused to admit that one signatory to a treaty could thus release itself from its obligations. "It has always been held that that right [to release a party to a treaty from its obligations] belongs only to the Governments who have been party to the original instrument." [7]

"The despatches of Prince Gortchakoff appear to assume that any one of the Powers who have signed the engagement may allege that occurrences have taken place which, in its opinion, are at variance with the provisions of the treaty, and, although this view is not shared or admitted by the co-signatory Powers, may found upon that allegation, not a request to these Governments for the consideration of the case, but an announcement to them that it has emancipated itself, or holds itself emancipated, from any stipulations of the treaty which it thinks fit to disapprove. Yet it is quite evident that the effect of such doctrine and of any proceeding which, with or without avowal, is founded upon it, is to bring the entire authority and efficacy of treaties under the discretionary control of each of the Powers who may have signed them; the result of which would be the entire destruction of treaties in their essence. For whereas their whole object is to bind Powers to one another, and for this purpose each one of the parties surrenders a portion of its free agency, by the doctrine and proceeding now in question, one of the parties in its separate and individual capacity brings back the entire subject into its own control, and remains bound only to itself." [8]

The British Government were not (formally at least)

Buxton, *op. cit.*, p. 107.) There is a good treatment in Dascovici, *op. cit.*, pp. 230ff.

[7] Hertslet, *op. cit.*, Vol. III, p. 1899.

[8] Phillipson and Buxton, *op. cit.*, p. 110.

objecting to a consideration of a revision of the Treaty of Paris, concerning which a certain scepticism had long existed in high quarters.[9] What they questioned was the right of one party to a treaty to declare it void when it no longer suited its convenience. The Russian claim, if admitted as a precedent, might undermine the whole structure of international law by reducing contracts to a mere basis of temporary expediency. There could be no stability in the international relations of the Powers if it would be impossible to calculate upon the fulfilment of solemn obligations. In short, we have already before us, in the technical language of the chancelleries, what is now known as the doctrine that a treaty may be treated as "a scrap of paper," to be torn up when more important issues seem involved.

Von Bethmann-Hollweg's phrase carries its own condemnation. But yet there is something underlying his and Gortchakoff's point of view, which international law has long recognized. Treaties must not be permitted to develop the rigidity of sacrosanct and immutable laws, binding like shackles the free life of nations. They are agreements reached under certain definite conditions and when those conditions are radically altered the treaties must be either revised or given up; or else the situation becomes intolerable. If, therefore, a nation is called upon to fulfil its obligation under changed circumstances, it may, in international law, plead that the obligation no longer holds when the conditions of its acceptance do not exist. This theory of the relativity of treaties to the conditions for which they were drawn up has been expressed in concise form as a

[9] Gladstone stated in Parliament that Palmerston had always doubted the possibility of a lasting neutralization of the Black Sea. Clarendon had also been of this opinion. Cf. Hansard, *Parliamentary Debates*, Vol. 204, 3d Ser., p. 850. Phillipson and Buxton, *op. cit.*, p. 127.

principle of treaty-making. It is admitted by most jurists and by all the Governments of civilized states that "all treaties are concluded under the tacit condition of *rebus sic stantibus*,"[10] which means that they are valid only as long as the circumstances remain substantially as they were.

But the point at issue, in 1870 and in 1914, was not the maintenance of immutable obligations in a changing world. It was simply whether one of the parties to a contract could, by invoking a *rebus sic stantibus* clause or upon the still more urgent plea of necessity—which is also admitted as a valid plea—by itself alone denounce the contract, without the consent of the other parties concerned. It is hardly necessary to call attention to the fact that the same issue again confronts the civilized world today.

Such an act upon the part of a Government would correspond, in international law, with "direct action" in home affairs. For it ignores the constitutional machinery for making or modifying international law, just as the syndicalist ignores that for domestic legislation. It is true that the international machinery is as yet so imperfect and fragmentary as almost to invite violation of its rules. In the absence of a World Parliament there is no international framework except that supplied by the bureaucratic agencies of nonrepresentative foreign offices. It is the tradition of diplomacy to recognize this international bureaucracy in lieu of an international state and to regard its negotiated conclusions as binding in a closer sense than domestic law. And yet there is something in the very nature of most treaties which suggests their evasion. For international

[10] Oppenheim, *International Law* (5th ed. by Lauterpacht), Vol. I, pp. 738ff., and literature there cited. The discussion in Phillipson and Buxton, *op. cit.*, pp. 115-119, is good.

agreements are so difficult to reach that until recently there were relatively few that were not inflicted upon one state by another more powerful than itself. The denunciation of such treaties by their victims when sufficiently strong to violate them with impunity is open to the same kind of objection that one may raise to syndicalist tactics in the state. It tends towards anarchy. Yet it should not be forgotten that the underlying cause of most instances of direct action in either case is the failure of the national or international organization to provide adequate representative institutions through which the just demands of a minority or a less powerful or defeated state can be met. As things stand now, the substitute for an international court which should decide when obligations change is an agreement of the co-signatories. They are the judges whether any of them may be freed from a common convention. So, at least, runs the theory of international law; and its inadequacy is obvious.

It is when one considers situations such as this that the full import of Article 19 of the Covenant of the League of Nations becomes evident. That article, empowering the League Assembly to recommend the reconsideration of treaties which had become inapplicable because of changed circumstances, was the recognition of the doctrine of *rebus sic stantibus* in a multipartite treaty intended for universal application. Its purpose was to provide a machinery for the revision of treaties by orderly processes of law instead of by force or the threat of force. The failure to carry the principle incorporated into Article 19 into practice and to utilize the method for peaceful readjustment of treaty relations among nations is perhaps one of the causes of the present international lawlessness where statesmen are resorting to the procedure adopted by Prince Gortchakoff two generations ago.

Turning from these matters of legal theory to the practical diplomatic history of the incident in question, we run into a strange chapter of the chronicle of Russian diplomacy as preserved for us by the Imperial Archivist, Dr. Goriainow. In the archives of Petrograd dealing with this history, there are—or were—despatches from the Russian ambassador at Washington, Catacazy, which, if taken at face value, bring the United States momentarily into the incident in a way astonishing to Americans. The story, as Goriainow gives it, is to the effect that Mr. Hamilton Fish, Secretary of State under President Grant, learned incidentally of Gortchakoff's circular letter through a telegram from Vienna. The Alabama affair was on his hands at the time, and, welcoming a possible ally against England, he strongly took the side of Russia. The United States had not been a party to the Treaty of Paris, and Mr. Fish felt free to act aggressively. He gave Catacazy to understand that it was possible to contract an offensive and defensive alliance between the United States and Russia and send an American fleet into the Black Sea.[11]

Catacazy was advised to be prudent and not involve Russia by engagements with America, for much as the Czar's Government appreciated good friends it "did not wish to pull another Government's nuts from the fire." [12] This amazing interlude in the history of American seclusion from European affairs, which would have plunged the United States into the tangled intrigue of its most persistent problem, the Eastern question, has found a place in

[11] Goriainow, op. cit., p. 194.
[12] Ibid., pp. 194, 195.

the sober pages of Goriainow; and, from there, has been summarized in the otherwise cautious work of Phillipson and Buxton, who give it full credence.[18] But it rests entirely upon the despatches of a man whom Mr. Fish himself charged with direct and wilful falsehoods and whose recall was asked by Washington in order that Washington should not, as Mr. Fish put it, be regarded as a home of intrigue, such as Constantinople. Whatever Mr. Fish said to Catacazy, it is inconceivable that he offered to force the issue with England by sending the American fleet through the Straits.[14]

The negotiations with other states need not be mentioned here. The result of Gortchakoff's letter was a conference at London, January, 1871. Granville began business by securing a declaration on the inviolability of treaties, which preserved the British doctrine while serving as a preamble to the action Russia was demanding:

"The plenipotentiaries of North Germany, of Austria-Hungary, of Great Britain, of Italy, of Russia and of Turkey, assembled today in conference, recognize that it is an essential principle of the law of nations that no Power can liberate itself from the engagements of the treaty, nor modify the stipulations thereof, unless with the consent of the contracting Powers by means of an amicable arrangement." [15]

After several failures to secure a statement acceptable to all [16] the Treaty of London was finally accepted,

[18] Cf. p. 112.

[14] Cf. *Senate Document* 5, 42nd Congress, 2d Session, for correspondence relative to Catacazy's dismissal.

[15] *Accounts and Papers*, Vol. 83 (1878), C. 1953, p. 57.

[16] *Accounts and Papers*, Vol. 83 (1878), summarized in Phillipson and Buxton, *op. cit.*, pp. 122–127.

March 13, 1871. The articles relating to the Straits and the Black Sea are as follows:

"Article I. Articles XI, XIII and XIV of the Treaty of Paris of the 30th March, 1856, as well as the special convention concluded between Russia and the Sublime Porte, and annexed to the said Article XIV, are abrogated, and replaced by the following article.

"Article II. The principle of the closing of the Straits of the Dardanelles and the Bosphorus, such as it has been established by the separate convention of the 30th March, 1856, is maintained, with power to His Imperial Majesty the Sultan to open the said Straits in time of peace to vessels of war of friendly and allied Powers, in case the Sublime Porte should judge it necessary in order to secure the execution of the stipulations of the Treaty of Paris of the 30th March, 1856.

"Article III. The Black Sea remains open, as heretofore, to the mercantile marine of all nations.

"Article VIII. The high contracting parties renew and confirm all stipulations of the Treaty of the 30th March, 1856, as well as of its annexes, which are not annulled or modified by the present treaty."

An additional convention between Russia and Turkey stated:

"Article I. The special convention concluded at Paris between His Majesty the Emperor of all the Russias and His Imperial Majesty the Sultan on the 18/30th March, 1856, relative to the number and force of the vessels of war of the two high contracting parties in the Black Sea, is and remains abrogated." [17]

[17] Hertslet, *op. cit.*, Vol. III, p. 1924.

The Treaty of London left the Straits closed as under the treaties of 1841 and 1856, but enlarged the Sultan's power to open them to friendly Governments if he thought it necessary in order to preserve the unrevoked articles of 1856.[18] On the other hand, Russia could have its fleets on the Black Sea, which was no longer neutralized. Prohibitions were removed at both the Straits and on the Black Sea.

[18] It will be recalled that from 1841 the Sultan had been prohibited allowing ships of war in time of peace.

VII

THE TREATY OF BERLIN, 1878

The Russo-Turkish War

BARELY was the ink dry on the Treaty of London when a Balkan crisis, resulting from the insurrection in the Turkish province of Herzegovina in July, 1875, once more directed the attention of the Great Powers to Constantinople and the Straits. After two years of diplomatic effort to localize the conflict in the Balkans,[1] Russia declared war against Turkey on April 24, 1877, and her apparent intention to utilize Turkey's embarrassment for a solution of the Straits question favorable to Russian interests almost resulted in a war between Russia and Great Britain.

The conduct of Russia, both before and after the outbreak of the Russo-Turkish war, as appears from contemporary records, indicates clearly that she was determined to reopen the question of the Straits. It is equally clear that British foreign policy, despite division of opinion at home and a rather vocal opposition to war, was firmly determined to

---

[1] These efforts culminated in the unsuccessful Constantinople Conference of the Great Powers, lasting from December, 1876, to January, 1877. For diplomatic correspondence relating to the convocation and aftermath of the Conference, see *British and Foreign State Papers*, Vol. 68, pp. 1064–1110; for the records of the meetings, see *ibid.*, pp. 1114–1207.

oppose alteration of the *status quo*, at least so far as Constantinople and the Straits were concerned,[2] while the other Powers—Austria-Hungary, France, Germany, and Italy—held aloof, at least on the surface. British anxiety over Russia's intention was manifested several months before Russia embarked upon the war; it was doubtless to allay such anxiety that Czar Alexander II, in a conversation with Lord Loftus, the British Ambassador to Russia, at Livadia on November 2, 1876, gave assurances that he neither wished nor intended to possess Constantinople.[3]

England did not wait long, after the outbreak of the war, to make her position clear. In a despatch dated May 6, 1877, Russia was informed that the British Government was not prepared to look with indifference on the passing of Constantinople into other hands. Allusion was made to serious objections, presumably on Great Britain's part, to any material alteration of existing regulations concerning navigation in the Straits. The Russian reply to these representations, dated May 30 and delivered to the British Foreign Secretary, Lord Derby, by Count Schouvalow, the Russian Ambassador to Great Britain, on June 8, was not very specific. Prince Gortchakoff assured the English that the Emperor did not contemplate the acquisition of Constantinople, and expressed the view that the question of the Straits should be settled "by a common agreement on equitable and efficiently

----

[2] For an instructive monograph on the conflict between Russia and Great Britain during this period, see Wirthwein, *Britain and the Balkan Crisis 1875–1878* (New York, 1935).

For the records of the diplomatic battle prior to the Congress of Berlin fought between Russia and Great Britain, see the British *Sessional Papers*, 1877, Vols. 89, 90 and 91; 1878, Vols. 81, 82 and 83. See also Hansard, *Parliamentary Debates* (3rd Ser.), Vols. 232–34 (1877); 237–42 (1878).

[3] See *London Gazette, Supplement,* issue of November 21, 1876.

guaranteed bases." [4] And lest England should attach greater importance to these assurances than they deserved, Count Schouvalow stated, in handing the reply to Lord Derby, that, for military reasons, the Russian Government could not pledge itself to refrain from *occupying* Constantinople; at the same time, he said that Russia would under no circumstances *remain* there, and the question of the Straits would be settled by agreement between the Great Powers. [5]

Following the fall of Plevna on December 1, 1877, and the consequent likelihood of Russian victory, Great Britain again made representations through the Russian Ambassador at London. He was informed, on December 13, of England's hope that Russia would not attempt to occupy, even temporarily, Constantinople and the Straits. [6] Again, Russia made an inconclusive answer, reserving for herself full liberty of action. The warning was repeated in January, 1878, following further Russian advance on the Balkan front (i.e., the taking of the Shipka Pass) and the rejection by the Russian Army Command of an armistice sought by Turkey. [7] On January 14, 1878, Lord Loftus, upon instructions of the British Government, informed Prince Gortchakoff that no modification of the treaties of 1856 and 1871 would be regarded as valid unless approved by all the signatory Powers. [8]

By this time it became apparent that Great Britain alone, among the Great Powers, was sufficiently concerned in the preservation of the *status quo* around Constantinople to

[4] *Sessional Papers*, 1877, Vol. 89, Russia #2; *British and Foreign State Papers*, Vol. 68, pp. 867, 869.
[5] *Sessional Papers*, 1878, Vol. 81, Turkey #15, No. 1.
[6] *Ibid.*, Turkey #3, No. 1.
[7] *Ibid.*, No. 3.
[8] *Ibid.*, No. 6.

challenge Russia on the new order she intended to establish. France did not manifest much interest, while Germany and Austria-Hungary, for reasons of their own,[9] were inclined to regard Russia's advance with benevolent indifference. As a matter of fact, a circular invitation of Turkey to the Powers, dated December 12, 1877, to offer their good offices and mediation, was cold-shouldered by Austria and expressly declined by the German Emperor. In spite of lack of support, Great Britain viewed the possible occupation of Constantinople and the Straits with extreme concern, and endeavored, by diplomatic action, to forestall Russia from dictating terms to a defeated Turkey and to prepare the ground for an international conference where these matters could be discussed. At the same time, she was apparently prepared to take action singlehanded and to abandon the "conditional" neutrality heretofore adopted, in order to safeguard her repeatedly expressed interests in that region.[10]

On January 23, after the fall of Adrianople and the march toward Gallipoli, the British Mediterranean fleet, anchored near Smyrna, was ordered to proceed to Constantinople, unless otherwise instructed at Besika, and to force passage

[9] Germany seems to have adopted a hands-off attitude in return for Russian neutrality in the Austro-Prussian and Prussian-Danish wars of 1866 and in the Franco-Prussian war of 1870. Bismarck felt that German interests could be safeguarded, if needed, through Austria-Hungary which by this time had abandoned its former anti-Prussian policy. Austria-Hungary, on the other hand, relied on a secret understanding with Russia, arrived at during a meeting of Alexander II and Francis Joseph at Reichstadt on July 8, 1876, and formally concluded on January 15, 1877, securing Russia's consent to Austrian plans for the occupation of the Turkish provinces of Bosnia, Herzegovina and Novibazar, against Austria's disinterestedness in Russian penetration elsewhere in the Balkans.

[10] Cf. the Queen's address to Parliament on January 17, 1878, and the debate on the answer, Hansard, *Parliamentary Debates* (3rd Ser.), Vol. 237, pp. 2ff.

through the Straits, if necessary. Upon a garbled telegram from the British Ambassador to Turkey that the conditions of preliminary peace agreed to between the Russian and Turkish negotiators provided for the settlement of the question of the Straits "by the Congress [of the Great Powers] and the Emperor of Russia" [11] and upon the receipt, on January 24, of Prince Gortchakoff's reassuring reply to the British representations that Russia did not intend to decide alone questions which were of interest to other Powers,[12] the order to the fleet was countermanded and Admiral Hornby anchored at Besika Bay.

Nevertheless, the British Government continued preparations for any eventuality. The bases of peace proposed by Russia, as revealed to the House of Commons on January 28, foresaw, *inter alia*, "an ulterior understanding for safeguarding the rights and interests of Russia in the Straits" [13]—which, to say the least, appeared somewhat vague in British eyes.

The signing of the armistice between Russia and Turkey on January 31, 1878, instead of diminishing, further increased England's suspicions. When the final terms became known to the British Government on February 8, Admiral Hornby was instructed to send a squadron to Constantinople at once. Russia and the neutral Powers were notified that this step was taken as a precautionary measure to protect British life and property.[14] Russia replied by announcing that she was equally entitled to protect Christians, and planned to send some troops into Constantinople for that purpose. The resulting acute tension was relaxed a few

[11] As subsequently established, the text read "by the Sultan and the Emperor," *Sessional Papers*, 1878, Vol. 81, Turkey #3, No. 34.

[12] *Ibid.*, No. 39.

[13] Hansard, *Parliamentary Debates* (3rd Ser.), Vol. 237, p. 540.

[14] *Ibid.*, p. 1331.

days later by a compromise, in which Russia promised not to occupy Constantinople and Gallipoli, and England promised not to land troops on either the European or Asiatic coast of the Dardanelles.[15]

By the time the preliminary peace between Russia and Turkey was signed at San Stefano on March 3, 1878,[16] the diplomatic line-up had changed to Russia's disadvantage. Austria-Hungary had definitely become fearful of excessive Russian ambitions and increasingly inclined to side with Great Britain in the latter's effort to check Russia. In view of Turkey's defeat, there was no prospect, short of war, of preventing the alteration, to a greater or a less extent, of the *status quo* in the Balkans which Russia sought to bring about. The objective of diplomatic activity shifted, therefore, to off-setting Russian dominance in that region. Thus, both Great Britain and Germany lent a sympathetic ear to hints from Vienna that occupation of some Balkan provinces of European Turkey by Austria-Hungary might effectively counterbalance enhanced Russian prestige in the peninsula.

Meanwhile, preparations were made for a conference of the Powers, which Austria first invited to Vienna but later consented to have meet at Berlin. The terms of the Treaty of San Stefano were examined in lengthy despatches exchanged between the various courts. While the provision relating to the Straits, inserted in the treaty, was innocuous enough,[17] the obvious intent of Russia to gain a foothold in

---

[15] *Sessional Papers*, 1878, Vol. 81, Turkey #17.

[16] For text, see *British and Foreign State Papers*, Vol. 69, p. 732; *Sessional Papers*, 1878, Vol. 83, Turkey #22; *United States Foreign Relations*, 1878, p. 866.

[17] Art. 24 provided that the Straits shall remain open, both in time of peace and in war, to neutral merchant ships going to and coming from Russian (Black Sea) ports, and that Turkey will not establish fictitious blockades against Russian ports in the Black Sea and the Sea

the Balkans through what amounted to a Russian protectorate over an oversized Bulgaria was not looked upon favorably by the other Powers.[18] It was feared that once Russia had established herself in the comparative proximity of Constantinople, she would be able to gain control over the Straits as well.[19]

A few days before the Congress met, Great Britain strengthened her position considerably: first, by entering into an understanding with Russia, at the end of May, which secured in advance concessions to be made by Russia at the conference; further, by concluding with Turkey, on June 4, 1878, a defensive alliance.[20] England promised military assistance to Turkey in case Russia should attempt to take away any Turkish territory in Asia beyond that to be fixed by the definitive treaty of peace. (Art. 1) In order to enable England to make necessary provision for executing her engagement, Turkey assented "to assign the Island of Cyprus to be occupied and administered by England." (Art. 2)[21]

---

of Azow, contrary to the spirit of the Declaration of Paris of 1856. *British and Foreign State Papers*, Vol. 69, p. 732, at p. 742; *United States Foreign Relations*, 1878, p. 866, at p. 871.

[18] In the light of recent developments, it is perhaps appropriate to point out that Bulgarian sympathies for Russia and the wide-spread inclination of the Bulgarian people to look upon Russia as the protector of Bulgarian interests date back to the attempt of Russia in 1878 to lay the foundations for a Greater Bulgaria. The dream of a Bulgarian empire was never abandoned, although the popularity of Russia was eclipsed following the Balkan wars in 1912–13.

[19] For the diplomatic correspondence between the Powers concerning the preparation of the Berlin Congress, see *British and Foreign State Papers*, Vol. 69, pp. 794–849.

[20] *Ibid.*, p. 744.

[21] The conditions under which England was to occupy and administer Cyprus were laid down in an Annex signed on July 1, 1878. *Ibid.*, p. 746.

THE CONGRESS OF BERLIN

It was after such preliminaries that a brilliant assemblage of Europe's leading statesmen met in Berlin on June 13, 1878, to settle the "affairs in the East." The list of participants was indeed impressive and indicative of the importance which was attached to the issues to be discussed. Germany's chief delegate was Prince Bismarck, who played the self-assumed rôle of the "honest broker" with astute, although somewhat relentless, diplomacy. Russia was represented by Prince Gortchakoff and Count Schouvalow, while Great Britain sent the Earl of Beaconsfield and Lord Salisbury. While they were the chief actors, the rôle played by Count Andrássy, the Austro-Hungarian Foreign Minister, was by no means negligible. The Foreign Ministers of France and Italy, Waddington and Corti, however, remained distinctly in the background. Contrary to recent practice where the prospective victim is not even given a hearing, the Berlin Congress adhered to nineteenth century diplomatic usages by allowing Turkey representation on a basis of theoretical equality, although in fact, of course, the function of the Turkish delegate was merely to receive what had already been decided.

After a month of arduous labor, the Treaty of Berlin was signed on July 13, 1878.[22] The provision relating to naviga-

---

[22] For the text, see *British and Foreign State Papers,* Vol. 69, p. 862; English text in *United States Foreign Relations,* 1878, p. 895. For the full records of the formal meetings, see *Sessional Papers,* 1878, Vol. 83, Turkey #39. A convenient collection of all important documents was published by the French Ministry for Foreign Affairs: *Documents diplomatiques. Affaires d'Orient. Congrés de Berlin,* 1878. (Paris, 1878) See also Cumming, A. N., "The Secret History of the Treaty of Berlin," *Nineteenth Century,* Vol. 58 (1905), p. 83.

tion of neutral merchant ships in the Straits, which Russia inserted in Art. 24 of the Treaty of San Stefano, did not reappear in the Treaty of Berlin; instead, Art. 63 of the Berlin treaty simply affirmed the *status quo ante* as determined by the treaties of 1856 and 1871.[23]

The Greater Bulgaria projected in the Treaty of San Stefano was shorn of most of its greatness; on the other hand, the provinces of Bosnia and Herzegovina were entrusted to Austria "for occupation and administration," [24] and the occupation of Cyprus by Great Britain was also confirmed. Thus, while Turkey was considerably weakened, Russia emerged from the Congress with far fewer fruits of her success on the battlefields than she had hoped to harvest. Although she had come physically closer to gaining control over the Straits than at any time before or since, once more she found herself blocked in her search for an outlet to the open seas through the Dardanelles.

While the Berlin Congress thus maintained the *status quo* around Constantinople, it by no means solved the question of the Straits, which merely became dormant for a generation. In some respects, the accomplishments of the Congress are indeed remarkable in that, as Professor Lord has pointed out, it was the only instance in the nineteenth century "when the Concert of Powers has been strong enough to bring a victorious belligerent to the bar of Europe and oblige him to submit the results of his victory to the judgment and re-

[23] Art. 24 of the Treaty of San Stefano was discussed at the meeting of July 6. See Protocol No. 14, *British and Foreign State Papers*, Vol. 69, pp. 1027-29.

[24] Art. 25 of the Berlin Treaty; see also Protocol No. 8 of June 28, *British and Foreign State Papers*, Vol. 69, p. 947; and Protocol No. 12 of July 4, *ibid.*, p. 1002.

vision of a Congress." [25] On the other hand, the seeds of future complications were planted, directly or indirectly, in the arrangements arrived at. This is certainly true with respect to the Austrian expansion into the Balkans which more than anything else irritated the Italians. The rekindling of Italian irredenta and the sour dissatisfaction of the Italians at being always ignored, which has since become almost an obsession with them (not wholly unjustified), are definitely traceable to the Berlin Congress.[26] France, which, like Italy, left Berlin empty-handed, was less irritated; for her acquiescence in British acquisition of Cyprus, Waddington received the assurances of Beaconsfield that England was disinterested in French aspirations in Tunis. Thus, the Berlin Congress was not merely a milestone in the contemplated partition of Turkey, but it marked also the starting point of a new wave of colonial expansion by foreshadowing the impending partition of North Africa. While these implications have no direct bearing on the question of the Straits, they nevertheless ought not to be ignored; for in laying the foundations for future clashes of interests, they were instrumental in leading to situations in which the question was bound to reappear in one shape or another. However, for the time being at least, Russia found herself once more

[25] Robert Howard Lord, "The Congress of Berlin," in *Three Peace Congresses of the Nineteenth Century* (Cambridge, Mass., 1917), p. 48. Of course this success was due to the fact that only Russia was weakened by war, while the other Great Powers were ready, both militarily and economically, to engage with fresh forces in a war if necessary. One is inevitably led to contemplate the possibilities of a negotiated peace in the present conflict under the moderating influence of powerful neutral nations, like the United States, Italy, Spain, and Turkey, if the war remains localized and one or the other of the belligerent parties should obtain a decisive victory.

[26] Concerning Italian resentment, see a thoughtful report in *United States Foreign Relations*, 1878, p. 475.

blocked in her ambition to gain control of the Straits, and her experiences at the Congress of Berlin were responsible perhaps as much as any other factor in turning her attention to the Far East.[27]

[27] For a brief but useful analysis of the Congress and the Treaty, see Woodward, E. L., *The Congress of Berlin, 1878.* (London, 1920) [Handbook prepared under the Direction of the Historical Section of the Foreign Office—No. 154.]

VIII

DIPLOMACY BEFORE THE WORLD WAR

THE INTERVAL OF QUIET

THE thirty years which elapsed between the Treaty of Berlin (1878) and the annexation of Bosnia and Herzegovina by Austria-Hungary (1908) were replete with diplomatic moves and countermoves on the part of the Great Powers, resulting ultimately in their realignment into the two combinations of the Triple Alliance and the Triple Entente and reflected in their jockeying for position in the Balkans. Yet the records show that throughout the greater part of this period none of the Powers sought actively to disturb the *status quo* in that region. The secret agreement signed at Berlin on June 18, 1881, by the representatives of Austria-Hungary, Germany and Russia, commonly known as the "League of the Three Emperors," sought to insure the *status quo* in the Balkans in general and the territorial integrity of European Turkey in particular, conditioned upon the maintenance of the régime of the Straits as laid down in the treaties of 1856 and 1871. In this respect the stipulations of Article 3 of the secret agreement were specific and unequivocal:

"The Three Courts recognize the European and mutually obligatory character of the principle of the closing of the Straits of the Bosphorus and of the Dardanelles, founded on international law, confirmed by treaties, and summed up in the declaration of the second Plenipotentiary of Russia at the session of July 12 of the Congress of Berlin (Protocol 19).

"They will take care in common that Turkey shall make no exception to this rule in favor of the interests of any Government whatsoever, by lending to warlike operations of a belligerent Power the portion of its Empire constituted by the Straits.

"In case of infringement, or to prevent it if such infringement should be in prospect, the Three Courts will inform Turkey that they would regard her, in that event, as putting herself in a state of war towards the injured Party, and as having deprived herself of the benefits of the security assured to her territorial *status quo* by the Treaty of Berlin." [1]

In a separate protocol, signed the same date, Austria-Hungary reserved the right to annex Bosnia and Herzegovina, which she occupied and administered by authorization of the Congress of Berlin, "at whatever moment she shall deem opportune." [2] Although the reappearance of the question of the Straits in 1908 was connected, as will presently appear, with the execution of this reserved right, there is no evidence either in the 1881 treaty or in subsequent diplomatic exchanges that Russia made any express or implied reservation that the anticipated or any other change in the Balkan *status quo* would revive her aspiration to control the Straits. Indeed the agreements (most of them secret) concluded between the Great Powers in the 1880's and 1890's, including the Triple Alliance and the Franco-Russian entente, seem to indicate that no change in the régime of the Straits was contemplated, although there was considerable bargain-

[1] Pribram, A. F., *The Secret Treaties of Austria-Hungary, 1879–1914,* Vol. 1 (Cambridge, Mass., 1920), p. 37.
[2] *Ibid.,* p. 43.

ing to define "spheres of interest" in anticipation of possible shifts elsewhere in the Balkan peninsula.[3]

But while the issue was dormant, it was by no means dead. Documents recently published in Soviet Russia [4] reveal that, despite formal agreements and assurances, the Imperial Government never ceased planning for the realization of the dream first conceived by Peter the Great. Thus, Mr. Nelidow submitted to Czar Alexander III a memorandum in 1882, just before his appointment as Russian Ambassador to Turkey, in which he examined Russia's position in great detail. The premise on which his analysis was based, and which was approved by the Czar, was that Russian control of the Straits was an historical necessity. It was only through such control that Russian political, military and commercial interests could be safeguarded and Austrian expansion in the Balkans could be checked. Nelidow urged that Russia must be prepared to forestall at any moment occupation of the Straits by a foreign power. As to the ultimate objective—the acquisition of the Straits by Russia—Nelidow foresaw three alternatives: war, intervention in internal troubles, or cooperation—even an alliance with Turkey. In order to avoid complications, he suggested that Constantinople should be a free city (naturally under Russian control). Though circumstances offered no opportunity for the realization of

[3] The secret agreements between Austria-Hungary, Germany, Great Britain, Italy and Russia are printed in Pribram, *loc. cit.*, note (1).

[4] Unfortunately, one of the most important documentary sources for students of Russian foreign policy in the pre-revolutionary era, namely the Red Archives (*Krasny Arkhiv*), is available only in the Russian language. Vols. 18 and 46-48 cover the period under review. For an excellent analysis of Russian aspirations in the Straits during these years, based largely on the above-cited documentary sources, see Mandelstam, "La politique Russe d'accès à la Méditerranée au XXème siècle," 47 *Recueil des cours* (1934, I), *Académie de droit international*, pp. 603ff., especially pp. 616-655.

any of these three alternatives, it is reasonable to assume that during the fifteen years Nelidow served as Russian Ambassador to Turkey, he kept in mind what he and his imperial master regarded as the historic mission of Russia. Indeed when, following the Armenian massacres in 1895–96, an intervention by the Great Powers in Turkey appeared likely, Nelidow suggested that preparations should be made for the occupation of the northern end of the Bosphorus by the Russian Black Sea fleet. While the Russian Government instructed Nelidow to seek a peaceful solution of the crisis in cooperation with the representatives of the other interested Powers at Constantinople, he was authorized directly to request the commander of the Black Sea fleet to despatch ships and landing troops in case of urgency.[5] Not willing to strain her relations with the other Powers, and particularly with France, no such action as urged by Nelidow was undertaken by Russia to secure control of the Straits.

It was during these years of comparative quiet that the question of the Straits as a problem of European concern was further complicated by the appearance on the scene of a new actor whose interest in the Near East had theretofore been academic—namely, Germany. Prussia never was concerned with the Near East, and up to the establishment of the Reich it was the Habsburg Monarchy which was the exponent of the policy of *Drang nach Osten*. Bismarck himself seems to have been satisfied to leave to Austria the protection of German interests in that region. But in the years following the Berlin Congress, Germany herself became the self-appointed standard-bearer of the *Drang nach*

[5] For a summary of Nelidow's memorandum of November 30, 1896, and the conclusions of the Crown Council of December 5, 1896, see Mandelstam, *op. cit.*, pp. 622–26.

Osten. Her appearance as one of the contestants was facilitated by England's loss of the popularity which she had acquired in Turkey by her determined opposition to Russian ambitions in 1877–78. After the occupation of Cyprus, the Turks no longer felt that Great Britain championed their cause unselfishly, and the return to power in 1880 of Gladstone, who was never regarded as friendly to Turkey, as well as the occupation of Egypt in 1882, had a decidedly adverse effect on British-Turkish relations. Germany appeared at the right moment to take the place in Turkish affections which Great Britain forfeited. The first step was the despatch of a German military mission, headed by Baron von der Goltz, to reorganize the Turkish army. In November, 1889, Emperor William II of Germany visited the Sultan at Constantinople, heralding a new era of German-Turkish relations. During the next decade there was rapid economic penetration of Turkey by German industry, commerce and finance, of which the establishment of a branch of the Deutsche Bank of Berlin in Constantinople bore witness. In 1898, another visit by the German Emperor to the Sultan resulted in the concession of the port of Haidar-Pascha to the German Anatolian Railways Company: the first concrete step toward the realization of the Berlin-Bagdad railway scheme. The *Drang nach Osten* was no longer a dream but a tangible reality. German ambitions, however, were of a different character from those of her predecessor in this policy. The aims of Austria were in their nature negative or passive. The Austrian objective was domination of the peninsula not for the sake of domination but in order to forestall domination by Russia which would expose the very existence of the Dual Monarchy to the danger of being surrounded on three sides by a Slav or Slav-controlled empire.

The policy was directed against Russia, but it did not carry with it the desire or necessity to control Constantinople and the Straits, and it certainly did not look further beyond to the East. On the other hand, the German *Drang nach Osten* was transformed into an affirmative, dynamic policy of expansion which conflicted not merely with Russian ambitions in the Straits but also with French and British vested interests in Asiatic Turkey and French political interests in Syria, and touched upon British interests in the Islamic world and India.

To be sure, Germany sought to allay, especially as far as Russia was concerned, any apprehension that her aspirations were other than economic. However, German professions of innocence did not change the increasing stronghold of Germany in the Near East; nor was Germany inclined to tie her hands. True, the German Emperor assured Czar Nicholas II that Germany had no intention of interfering with Russia in the Straits. But when, following the concession granted to the German Anatolian Railways Company, Russia, fearful of German penetration, proposed in March, 1899, an understanding concerning the Straits and the Near East, Germany declined to enter into any formal agreement. Chancellor Bülow told Count Osten-Sacken, the Russian Ambassador at Berlin, that no such agreement was necessary in view of the fact that Germany had no desire either to intervene in Balkan affairs or to exercise an "exclusive influence" in Constantinople, where Germany had no future ambitions; particularly, she would never cross Russia's path in the Straits.[6]

[6] For diplomatic correspondence relating to the proposed Russo-German understanding, see *Die Grosse Politik der europäischen Kabinette, 1871–1914* (hereafter cited: *Die Grosse Politik*), Vol. 14, Pt. II, Chap. 95, pp. 531ff.

A radical solution of the question of the Straits was envisaged by Count Mouraview, the Russian Foreign Minister, early in 1900; the moment seemed opportune in view of the Boer War, which was occupying and embarrassing England sufficiently at that time to preclude effective opposition on her part to action by Russia. But internal conditions, particularly lack of naval preparedness and financial difficulties, made the execution of any such plan inadvisable. Moreover, the attention of Russia was being directed increasingly to the Far East, where she soon became engaged in war with Japan. France and England, meanwhile, were endeavoring to compose by negotiation and conference various differences with Germany and Russia, and with each other. Thus, because of an interplay of circumstances, conflicts between the Great Powers with respect to the Straits were submerged for several years.

But when Russia, defeated by Japan in Asia and further weakened by revolution at home, turned her attention anew to Europe and the Near East, the stage was set for her ambitious Foreign Minister, Mr. Izvolski, to rekindle the smouldering question into a burning flame.

THE ANGLO-RUSSIAN AGREEMENT AND THE REOPENING OF THE QUESTION OF THE STRAITS

Following her defeat in the war with Japan, Russia sought to strengthen her position by putting on a friendlier basis her relations with Great Britain which, to a greater or less extent, had been strained by the imperial ambitions of both governments not only in the Near East but in Asia. Such a policy had been urged upon Russia for some time by her French ally, but it was not until after the Japanese war that she was inclined to listen. An additional influence upon Russian policy lay in the fact that during the Russo-Japanese war she for the first time felt seriously handicapped by the prohibition of passage through the Straits, a prohibition which England, the ally of Japan, insisted on maintaining.

Negotiations for a settlement of conflicting interests between Russia and England began in 1906 and led to the conclusion of an agreement, signed at St. Petersburg on August 31, 1907, concerning Persia, Afghanistan and Tibet, which made possible the Triple Entente of England, Russia and France.[7] In the course of these negotiations Russia reopened the question of the Straits in the expectation that a revision of the nineteenth century treaties might be made part of the general settlement. There was indication of Russian intention to raise the issue as early as March, 1906,[8] but

[7] For the diplomatic background of the Anglo-Russian rapprochement and the negotiations leading to the St. Petersburg agreement, see *British Documents on the Origins of the War, 1898–1914* (hereafter cited: *British Documents*), Vol. IV, Chaps. XXV, XXVI, sec. II, XXVII, sec. IV, XXVIII. For the text of the agreement, see *ibid.*, p. 618; *British and Foreign State Papers*, Vol. 100, p. 555; *British Treaty Series*, 1907, No. 34.

[8] In a private letter, dated March 1, 1906, Mr. Spring-Rice (later Sir Cecil), Counsellor of the British Embassy at St. Petersburg, reported to Sir Edward Grey, the British Foreign Secretary, that Russia desired to obtain England's assent to the interpretation of the Black Sea clause of the London Treaty of 1871 which Lord Salisbury advocated, but Count Schouvalow opposed at the Berlin Congress. In Salisbury's opinion, the clause meant only an engagement on the part of the European Powers to respect the independent determination of the Sultan in conformity with existing treaties; while according to Schouvalow, Russia regarded the clause as part of the law of nations and, therefore, independent of the decisions of the Sultan. Since Great Britain in practice acquiesced in this latter interpretation during the Russo-Japanese war (for the incident between England and Russia arising from the passage of the Russian volunteer fleet through the Straits, see *British Documents*, Vol. IV, pp. 41ff.), Russia felt that England ought no longer to object to the passage of Russian warships if this occurred with the permission of Turkey. *British Documents*, Vol. IV, No. 210, p. 226.

the matter was not actually broached until the end of November, 1906, in an interview between the Russian chargé d'affaires at London with Sir Charles Hardinge, Permanent Under-Secretary of State for Foreign Affairs. Hardinge evaded a direct reply by saying that the question of the Dardanelles was not a matter of interest for Russia and Great Britain alone,[9] but in a memorandum written by him a few days earlier, it appears that the British Foreign Office was inclined at that time to promise its support in obtaining some concessions for Russia on this point in return for other advantages.[10] This appears even more clearly from records of a conversation which Sir Edward Grey had with Count Benckendorff, the Russian Ambassador at London, on March 15, 1907. Count Benckendorff, without instructions from his Government, intimated to Grey that British acquiescence, in principle, in the opening of the Straits would have a favorable effect on pro-British tendencies in Russia. Grey replied that, in his opinion, the better relations with Russia which might be expected to result from the pending negotiations would require the abandonment of the prior British policy of closing the Straits, and expressed the fear that an agreement on the part of the Government to open

[9] *Ibid.*, No. 242, p. 254. Sir Edward Grey to Sir Arthur Nicolson (later Lord Carnock), British Ambassador to Russia, November 30, 1906.

[10] The memorandum dated November 16, 1906, and printed in *British Documents*, Vol. IV, pp. 58–60, stated: ". . . It is probable that the Russian Government will now desire a modification of the *status quo*, and if it is thought desirable to make some concession to Russia in return for other advantages to be obtained during the pending negotiations, and if this is a concession upon which they set store, it would be possible to promise to the Russian Government our support in obtaining the consent of the Powers to a modification of Article II of the Treaty of London in the sense of the declaration made by Lord Salisbury at the 18th Sitting of the Berlin Congress. . . ."

the Straits for Russia while keeping it closed to England would not be palatable to the British public. He asked for time to consider the matter and discuss it with the Prime Minister.[11] A few days later, Grey restated the views of the British Government to Benckendorff that "England must no longer make it a settled object of her policy to maintain the existing arrangement with regard to the passage of the Dardanelles." However, he doubted the expediency of asking England to make a definite engagement in this respect, both on account of public opinion in England and of the possibility of arousing the susceptibilities of other Powers, particularly France and Germany. If Russia nevertheless desired to raise the issue, the British Government was prepared to discuss it.[12]

Izvolski, the Foreign Minister, considered these statements, cautious as they were, as marking a "great evolution in the relations of the two countries."[13] In an undated memorandum which he handed to the British Ambassador on April 14, he summed up Russia's position as follows:[14] the Russian Government is gratified that closing of the Straits is no longer a cardinal point of British policy. It regards it as of the greatest importance that the British Foreign Secretary has not raised objection in principle to a contemplated arrangement under which Russian warships would have exclusive right of passage through the Straits,

[11] *British Documents*, Vol. IV, No. 257, p. 279. Sir Edward Grey's memorandum of March 15, 1907.

[12] *Ibid.*, No. 258, p. 280. Sir Edward Grey to Sir A. Nicolson, March 19, 1907.

[13] *Ibid.*, Nos. 259 and 261, pp. 281 and 283. Sir A. Nicolson to Sir Edward Grey, March 25 and March 27, 1907.

[14] *Ibid.*, p. 287, enclosure to No. 265. Sir A. Nicolson to Sir Edward Grey, April 14, 1907.

while the entry of the naval forces of other Powers in the
Black Sea would be prohibited.[15] The Russian Government feels, in the light of Sir Edward Grey's observations,
that it would be inopportune to conclude a special arrangement concerning the Straits during the negotiations in
course and, therefore, taking note of the attitude of the
British Government, reserves discussion of the question for
a more favorable time.

The implications which Izvolski sought to read into the
conversations of Count Benckendorff with the British Foreign Secretary apparently disturbed Sir Edward Grey and
he amplified his position in another memorandum dated
April 27.[16] He pointed out that his original proposal to discuss a revision of the régime of the Straits did not exclude
the right of exit being allowed to other Black Sea powers.
While Great Britain did not feel it incumbent on her to
raise that issue, she did not wish to have her hands tied,
should it be raised by other Powers. He also pointed out that
Izvolski's memorandum failed to take account of the fact
that the original proposal discussed between Grey and
Benckendorff contemplated opening the Straits on the same
terms for all Powers, thus implying entry into the Black
Sea by other Powers as well. He expressed satisfaction that
Russia agreed to defer discussion, and indicated that Eng-

---

[15] According to a note of Lord Fitzmaurice, Parliamentary Under-
Secretary of State for Foreign Affairs, "the Russian Government are
taking a most unfair advantage of the expressions used by Sir E. Grey
in his conversation with Count Benckendorff . . . and still more of his
judicious silence on certain points. An attempt is made to extract from
the latter an implied consent to Russian vessels of war having an *exclusive* right of exit, and to the denial of equal rights of entry to the
waters of the Black Sea to the ships of other Powers. . . ." *Ibid.*, p. 288.
[16] *Ibid.*, p. 290, enclosure to No. 268. Sir Edward Grey to Sir A.
Nicolson, May 1, 1907.

land's support would be forthcoming only if the Asiatic agreement proved to be workable.[17] These observations were noted in a memorandum of Izvolski, dated July 10, 1907,[18] with the exception of Grey's insistence that good relations in Asia were a preliminary condition to a discussion of the Straits.

Thus it is evident that while Great Britain was willing, in principle, to discuss the question of the Straits, neither Sir Edward Grey nor Izvolski committed himself to any particular solution; that both were mindful of the necessity of obtaining the consent of other Powers to any change in the existing regulations.

The Sandjak Railway Plan and the Buchlau Conversations

The next incident in the chain of events was the tension between Russia and Austria-Hungary resulting from the announcement in January, 1908, by Baron Aerenthal, the Foreign Minister of the Habsburg Monarchy, of the contemplated railway line through the Sandjak of Novibazar, occupied by Austria-Hungary since 1878. This plan, which was expected to link Bosnia-Herzegovina with the Turkish railroads and would also have given Austria a direct con-

---

[17] ". . . if the negotiations now in progress between the two Governments with regard to Asiatic questions had a satisfactory result, the effect upon British public opinion would be such as very much to facilitate a discussion of the Straits question *if it came up later on.* I have no doubt whatever that if, as a result of the present negotiations, the British and Russian Governments *remained* on good terms in Asia, the effect on British public opinion and on any British Government with regard to other questions, including this, would be very great." (Italics ours)

[18] *Ibid.*, p. 295, enclosure to No. 275. Sir A. Nicolson to Sir Edward Grey, July 10, 1907.

nection to Salonika, created consternation in Russia as an evidence of Austria's expansionist policy in the Balkans.[19] The situation was examined at a secret meeting of the Russian cabinet on February 3, 1908, at which Izvolski raised the question whether Russia should not, in the light of recent developments, abandon a defensive policy aiming at the preservation of the *status quo* in the Balkans and adopt an energetic affirmative policy directed toward the realization of Russia's historic mission in the Near East—possibly in cooperation with Great Britain. In the light of internal conditions and considering the slow progress made in military and naval preparations, the conclusion was reached that Russia was not yet sufficiently strong to pursue a policy which might lead to complications and to conflicts with the Great Powers interested in the Near East.[20] Thus the only method available for Izvolski was diplomatic bargaining.

At the beginning of July, 1908, he proposed to Austria-Hungary a discussion of the *status quo* in the Balkans and in the Straits in a "friendly spirit of reciprocity," without prejudice to the earlier position taken by the Russian Government that these were questions of general European concern and any change could be effected only with the consent of the Powers.[21] The Austrian reply of August 27 was encouraging: it suggested as the bases of understanding, an agreement that both Governments could, as long as cir-

[19] For the repercussions of the Sandjak railways plan, see *Die Grosse Politik*, Vol. 25, Part II, Chap. 187, and *British Documents*, Vol. V, Chap. 39, pp. 321ff.

[20] Mandelstam, *op. cit.*, pp. 656–62.

[21] The memorandum of Izvolski dated July 2, 1908, is printed in *Osterreich-Ungarns Aussenpolitik*, Vol. 1, No. 8, p. 9 and in *Die Grosse Politik*, Vol. 26, Pt. II, No. 9055.

cumstances permitted, continue a policy aiming at the maintenance of the *status quo* in Turkey. Should Austria-Hungary feel compelled to annex Bosnia and Herzegovina, Russia would adopt a friendly attitude. Austria, on her part, was disposed toward a confidential and friendly exchange of views concerning Constantinople and the Straits.[22]

The door having thus been opened to an understanding between Russia and Austria-Hungary, a meeting between the foreign ministers of the two countries was arranged. This meeting took place on September 16, 1908, at the country estate of Count Berchtold, Austro-Hungarian Ambassador to Russia, in Buchlau, Moravia. Although the conference had far-reaching consequences, no record of the conversations and no unimpeachable written evidence of the agreements reached between the two statesmen are available, except the conflicting versions of Izvolski and Aerenthal.[23] The substance of the questions discussed, it appears beyond doubt, were Russia's attitude toward the contemplated an-

[22] *Österreich-Ungarns Aussenpolitik*, Vol. 1, No. 48, p. 59.
[23] As to Aerenthal's version, see his notes (undated) on the Buchlau conversations in *Österreich-Ungarns Aussenpolitik*, Vol. 1, No. 79, pp. 86ff., and his letter of September 26, 1908, to von Bülow, the German Chancellor, in *Die Grosse Politik*, Vol. 26, Pt. I, No. 8934, p. 35. For Izvolski's interpretation of what occurred, see his memorandum (undated) handed to Sir F. (later Viscount) Bertie, British Ambassador to France, and communicated by the latter to Sir Edward Grey with despatch dated October 4, 1908, *British Documents*, Vol. V, No. 292, enclosure, p. 383; a private report, dated September 20, 1909, of Sir Fairfax Cartwright, British Ambassador at Vienna, on a conversation had with Izvolski in Venice, *ibid.*, No. 870, p. 807; Sir A. Nicolson's report from St. Petersburg, dated Nov. 10, 1909, to Sir Edward Grey, *ibid.*, No. 872, p. 810. See also the letter of the German Secretary of State for Foreign Affairs to Chancellor von Bülow, dated September 26, 1908, reporting his interview with the Russian Foreign Minister, *ibid.*, No. 8935, p. 39, and the sympathetic analysis of available records by Mandelstam, *op. cit.*, pp. 667–680. See also *Out of My Past. The Memoirs of Count Kokovtsov*, pp. 215–218.

nexation of Bosnia and Herzegovina by Austria-Hungary, the imminence of which seems to have been revealed to Izvolski by Aerenthal; and Austria's attitude toward the intention of Russia to raise the question of the Straits. The substance of the agreement reached seems to have been that Russia would acquiesce in the annexation on the promise of Austria to support Russia in her effort to have the Straits opened. But there is considerable difference as to the details. Aerenthal's version was that Izvolski agreed unconditionally to annexation, while Aerenthal conditioned Austria's support at the Straits on the consent of the interested Great Powers. Izvolski contended that he agreed to acquiesce in annexation only after warning Aerenthal of the dangers inherent in that step and provided that Austria-Hungary first secured the consent of the other signatories of the Treaty of Berlin of 1878.

IX

THE PRELUDE TO WAR

THE BOSNIAN CRISIS AND IZVOLSKI'S DIPLOMATIC DEFEAT

WHATEVER may have passed between the Russian and Austro-Hungarian Foreign Ministers at Buchlau, Baron Aerenthal proceeded promptly to annex Bosnia and Herzegovina, by proclamation on October 6, 1908, before Izvolski, who was touring European capitals, could secure the consent of the Great Powers to the opening of the Straits. It is doubtful whether Aerenthal's action, however much it may be criticized from other points of view, was in any way responsible for Izvolski's failure to secure such consent. In fact, his overtures in this respect to Baron von Schön, the German Under-Secretary for Foreign Affairs, whom he visited at Berchtesgaden a few days after the Buchlau meeting, and conversations with French statesmen in Paris resulted only in noncommittal replies. What was even more important, Great Britain, the chief opponent of Russia in this respect, was clearly unwilling to go beyond the position taken by Sir Edward Grey in his conversations with Count Benckendorff and the exchange of memoranda with Izvolski a year and a half earlier. England's reluctance alone would have been sufficient to frustrate Izvolski's plans, irrespective of anything which may have been agreed upon with Aerenthal.

Faced with a *fait accompli*, Izvolski, smarting under what he believed to be Aerenthal's treachery, sought to inflict a humiliation on Austria-Hungary by urging the convocation of a conference of the signatories of the Berlin Treaty to examine the situation created by the annexation of Bosnia and Herzegovina. However, the question of the Straits was not included in the agenda contemplated by Izvolski who, seeking to improve Russo-Turkish relations, desired to discuss the matter first with Turkey. In an interview in London with Grey on October 12, Izvolski sought unsuccessfully a promise that Great Britain would not oppose an arrangement, if one could be worked out between Russia and Turkey, under which warships of Russia and other Black Sea Powers should have the exclusive right of passage through the Straits, limited to three ships at a time and without right of stopping and anchoring.[1] Grey not only felt that raising the question at that moment was inopportune, but also doubted that such a one-sided arrangement, without reciprocal rights for other Powers at least in time of war, would be acceptable to the British public,[2] a point on which Grey insisted in conversations with Count Benckendorff in March, 1907. So one-sided an arrangement would mean that in case of war, Turkey being neutral, British maritime commerce could be harassed by warships of Black Sea Powers, permitted to pass through the Straits,

---

[1] Grey considered Izvolski's proposal as maintaining the principle of closure of the Straits subject to a limited servitude in favor of Russia and other Black Sea Powers. *British Documents*, Vol. V, No. 379, pp. 442–43. Sir E. Grey to Sir A. Nicolson, Oct. 14, 1908.

[2] *Ibid.*, No. 358, p. 424, and No. 364, p. 429. Sir E. Grey to Sir A. Nicolson, Oct. 12, 1908. Apparently, the British Cabinet was more opposed to any such solution of the Straits question than Grey. See *ibid.*, No. 372, pp. 434–35. Sir C. Hardinge to Sir A. Nicolson, Oct. 13, 1908.

while they could not be pursued into the Black Sea. Grey also was apprehensive that any further pressure put on Turkey, already beset with difficulties caused by the Bulgarian declaration of independence and by the action of Austria-Hungary, might have fatal consequences for the internal order and the integrity of that country. Izvolski then suggested that this fear might be assuaged by a provision that in time of war, Turkey being neutral, all belligerents would have equal facilities for passage through the Straits.[3] This suggestion seems to have appealed to Grey at least and he agreed to submit the modified proposal to the cabinet meeting.[4] The final position of the British Government, summed up by Grey in a memorandum dated October 14, 1908, did not advance Izvolski's plan a single inch beyond the already declared willingness of Great Britain to discuss the question at a favorable moment.[5] In view of the importance of this state paper, setting forth in clear language the attitude of the British Government, it deserves to be fully quoted:

"H[is] M[ajesty's] Government agree that the opening of the Straits is fair and reasonable, and in principle they will not oppose it.

[3] *Ibid.*, No. 371, pp. 433-34. Sir E. Grey to Sir A. Nicolson, Oct. 13, 1908.

[4] Hardinge believed that it might be accepted by the cabinet because the element of reciprocity might satisfy public opinion. ". . . From a strategical point of view, there is no possible advantage in our ships being able to go into the Black Sea in time of war. It is already a settled principle of naval warfare with us that in no case would our fleets enter the Straits, unless Turkey were our ally. The condition of reciprocity, however, is a shop-window ware, since the public do not understand these strategical considerations. . . ." *Ibid.*, No. 372, p. 435. Sir C. Hardinge to Sir A. Nicolson, Oct. 13, 1908.

[5] *Ibid.*, No. 377, p. 441.

"If the proposal made was that the Straits should be open on terms of perfect equality to all, the proposal would be one to which no exception could be taken.

"The difficulty arises from the proposal to give Russia and the riverain Powers an exclusive, though limited, right. H[is] M[ajesty's] Government cannot but feel that the time is very inopportune for securing general assent to such an arrangement.

"Feeling in England has very much resented the action of Austria; it would be greatly disappointed if Russia, after protesting against Austrian action, apparently used the occasion to secure an advantage for herself which had any appearance of prejudice to the position of Turkey, or altered the *status quo* to the disadvantage of others.

"If, on the other hand, there is cordial cooperation between Russia and England to overcome present difficulties on disinterested lines, the good effect on public opinion here would be very marked and would predispose it to a change about the Straits in a sense favourable to Russia.

"H[is] M[ajesty's] Government, however, agreeing in principle that some opening of the Straits is reasonable, cannot refuse to discuss the question.

"They feel that a purely onesided arrangement, which would give the Black Sea Powers in time of war the advantage of having the whole of the Black Sea as an inviolable harbour from which cruisers and commerce destroyers could issue and retire at will, free from pursuit by a belligerent, is not one for which public opinion in England is prepared or which it could be induced to accept.

"Any arrangement, therefore, must be one which, while giving Russia and the riverain Powers egress at all times under some such limited conditions as M. Isvolsky has indicated and securing them from menace or the establishment of foreign naval power in the Black Sea in time of peace, would yet contain such an element of reciprocity as would in the eventuality of war place belligerents on an equal footing with regard to the passage of the Straits.

"H[is] M[ajesty's] Government would further observe that the consent of Turkey would be a necessary preliminary to any proposal. To put pressure upon Turkey at this moment to make an arrangement which she might regard, however unreasonably, as a menace to her interests would defeat what we believe is the joint object of England and Russia, viz.: to prevent the overthrow of the present Turkish Government, and the confusion and anarchy which would probably result."

To soften Izvolski's reaction to this negative reply to his overtures, Grey assured Izvolski, in a private letter, that in insisting upon the difficulty of settling the question of the Straits at that time, he was not motivated by any desire to keep the Straits closed. On the contrary, he wrote, he positively desired "to see an arrangement made, which will open the Straits on terms which would be acceptable to Russia and to the riverain States of the Black Sea, while not placing Turkey or outside Powers at an unfair disadvantage. Some such arrangement seems to me essential to the permanent establishment of good-will between Russia and ourselves." [6] Although disappointed, Izvolski could not do anything but accept the defeat and return empty-handed to Saint Petersburg. Ultimately, even his plan for the conference came to naught on the opposition of Austria.

But while Aerenthal was thus not directly responsible for Izvolski's defeat, the controversy between the two statesmen had far-reaching consequences. It marked the definite estrangement between Austria-Hungary and Russia, manifested in the immediate adoption by Russia of a Balkan policy directed against Austria. While Izvolski did

[6] *Ibid.*, No. 387, pp. 451–52. Sir E. Grey to Mr. Izvolski, Oct. 15, 1908.

not long remain Foreign Minister of Russia, nevertheless, as Russian Ambassador to France, his activity, motivated by a persistent feeling of humiliation at the hands of the former Austro-Hungarian Foreign Minister, is frequently cited as one of the factors contributing to the World War.[7]

While still in office, Izvolski espoused on Russia's behalf, almost openly, the Serbian irredenta movement directed primarily against Austria-Hungary, and the rôle of protector of the Slav nations of the Balkans was increasingly emphasized to the detriment of both the Habsburg Empire and Turkey. Both policies were continued with more or less adroitness by Izvolski's successor, Sazonow. The problem was still studied as to how to secure a free hand for Russia when the expected disintegration of the Ottoman Empire should become a reality. Having been assured by Germany that she looked favorably upon Russian aspirations in the Straits,[8] Izvolski succeeded, just before leaving his post, in concluding a secret treaty at Racconigi with Italy, under which Italy agreed to maintain a benevolent attitude, should Russia raise the question of the Straits, in return for Russian acquiescence in Italian claims to Tripoli.[9]

[7] Stieve, *Isvolski and the World War*. Transl. by Dickes (1926). Izvolski did not, however, have the influence he claimed to have, as often happens in the case of statesmen who have lost power.

[8] For Germany's benevolent attitude toward Russia during the Bosnian crisis, motivated chiefly by her desire to embarrass Great Britain and to avert further rapprochement between England and Russia, see *Die Grosse Politik*, Vol. 26, Pt. I, Chap. 199, pp. 367ff. Concerning the Bosnian crisis see also Poincaré, *Au service de la France*, Vol. I, Chap. XI; Taube, *La politique russe d'avant-guerre et la fin de l'empire des Tsars* (Paris, 1928), pp. 173ff.

[9] Art. 5 of the agreement concluded at Racconigi on October 24, 1909, during a meeting of Nicolas II, with the King of Italy. Text in *Un livre noir*, Vol. I, pp. 357–58. It may be noted that Izvolski deliberately arranged the trip through a route avoiding Austrian territory, thus emphasizing the displeasure of Russia toward Austria-Hungary. For the background of the Racconigi meeting, see *Die Grosse Politik*, Vol. 27, Pt. I, Chap. 214; and *British Documents*, Vol. IX, *passim*.

This was followed by a secret military agreement with Bulgaria, concluded in December, 1909,[10] which has been regarded as a first step in clearing the way for the formation of a Balkan league—a league which, while holding Austria-Hungary in check, could also further weaken Turkey and so be instrumental in advancing Russia's position at the Straits.

THE ITALO-TURKISH AND BALKAN WARS

Opportunity for action was supplied by the outbreak of the Italo-Turkish war over Tripoli at the end of September, 1911. Russia felt that Italy, although not committed to any specific solution of the Straits question under the Racconigi agreement, could be counted upon not to oppose action which would further embarrass her enemy,[11] and began to explore the possibilities in the new situation.

Early in October, 1911, during Sazonow's illness, an informal proposal was initiated by Tcharykow, the Russian Ambassador to Turkey, for a convention of the Powers, to open the Straits, but it progressed very little on account of

---

[10] Text in Boghitchevitch, *Kriegsursachen* (Zurich, 1919), p. 115.

[11] Immediately after Italy's declaration of war, Izvolski, then Russian Ambassador to France, discussed with Tittoni, the Italian Ambassador to France, upon instructions from his Government, the possibility of establishing more precisely Italy's commitments to Russia concerning the Straits. Stieve, *op. cit.*, p. 38.

It is noteworthy—especially in the light of subsequent developments—that Italy, whose interests as a Mediterranean power *par excellence* would seem to require security against interference with her maritime commerce, unlike Great Britain showed no apprehension over the appearance of Russian warships in the Mediterranean. This may perhaps be explained on the ground that Italy, although a member of the Triple Alliance, counted on British naval support in case of complications in the Mediterranean. (The Triple Alliance had a clause exempting Italy from any obligation to fight England.)

Turkey's reluctance to enter into discussion, and was disavowed by Sazonow at the end of November, 1911—presumably because the reaction of the interested powers was,
to say the least, not enthusiastic. France, while grateful for
Russia's support in the Moroccan crisis,[12] not only had been
traditionally friendly to Turkey ever since the time of
Francis I, but also had varied interests in the Near East and
was reluctant to give a blank check to Russia.[13] Germany,
under the insistence of Baron Marshall, German Ambassador at Constantinople, whose skillful diplomacy drew
Turkey more and more within the German orbit (he even
succeeded in overcoming the temporary anti-German ten-
dency manifested by the Young Turks after the revolution),
abandoned the sympathetic attitude toward the Russian
project which the Emperor and Chancellor Bethmann-
Hollweg somewhat impulsively adopted at the outset.[14]
Finally, Great Britain was unwilling to go beyond the position taken in the fall of 1908, when the matter was discussed
between Sir Edward Grey and Izvolski.[15]

Meanwhile, a new alignment was taking place in the Balkans, although in the end its results did not bring Russia any
nearer to the Straits. The negotiations between Bulgaria
and Serbia which began early in October, 1911, a few days

[12] Neratow, in charge of the Russian Foreign Office during the illness
of the Minister, Mr. Sazonow, wrote on Oct. 5, 1911, to Izvolski that
"the time has come to assure ourselves of the agreement of our Ally not
to oppose our standpoint or any steps we may take," and suggested that
an agreement concerning the Straits might take the form of letters exchanged between the two Foreign Ministers, as was done with Italy at
Racconigi. Stieve, *op. cit.*, pp. 36–37.
[13] See *Documents diplomatiques français (1871–1914)*, 3rd Ser. (1911–
1914), Vol. I, particularly Nos. 18, 58, 88, 105, 114, 279, 322 and 433.
[14] See *Die Grosse Politik*, Vol. 30, Pt. I, Chap. 236, pp. 201ff.
[15] See *British Documents*, Vol. IX, Pt. I, Chap. 74, Sec. III, pp. 320ff.

after the outbreak of the Italo-Turkish war, with Russia's blessing, led to the conclusion of a treaty of alliance on February 29/March 13, 1912. A secret annex to the treaty provided for the partition, between the Balkan allies, of the greater part of European Turkey (specifically Macedonia), such partition to take place at an opportune moment. This annex also recognized Russia as the umpire over any controversy which might arise between the Allies.[16] This provision ensured to Russia the decisive word in any redistribution of territory and thus safeguarded by implication her interests in the region of the Straits. This alliance, to which subsequently Greece and Montenegro adhered, was of course concluded in anticipation of finding Turkey materially weakened by the war with Italy—a circumstance which could be utilized by the allied Balkan states to realize their ambitions which, in turn, would put Russia in a stronger position than ever before with reference to Turkey, Constantinople, and the Straits.[17]

The closure of the Straits by Turkey in April, 1912, following the attack by the Italian fleet on the Dardanelles, short-lived as it was, inflicted serious losses on Russian commerce and made Russia more conscious of the disadvantageous régime, from her own point of view, governing navigation through the Straits. Within a few years these disadvantages had been brought home to her twice: in the war with Japan her inability to get out her Black Sea fleet em-

[16] For the text of the treaty and of the secret annex, see *British Documents*, Vol. IX, Pt. I, p. 781.

[17] Interesting light on Russia's rôle in the creation of the Balkan alliance is thrown in *British Documents*, Vol. IX, Pt. I, Chap. 76, pp. 513ff. See also W. L. Langer, "Russia, the Straits Question and the Origins of the Balkan League," *Political Science Quarterly*, Vol. 43 (1928), pp. 321ff. See also Sir George Buchanan, *My Mission to Russia* (London, 1923), Vol. I, pp. 120–121; but cf. Taube, *op. cit.*, pp. 244ff.

barrassed Russia as a belligerent, while in the Italo-Turkish war she suffered as a neutral.

During the Balkan wars which followed, in 1912–1913, the question of the Straits was only incidentally discussed, although it loomed large in the background of Russian pre-occupations. When the rapidly advancing Bulgarian army was nearing Constantinople, Russia became apprehensive and notified London and Paris, as well as Sofia, that she was absolutely opposed to the entry of the Balkan allies into the Turkish capital—an opposition which she only reluctantly withdrew in view of their unexpected victories. The fear that another power might dominate the Straits caused Russia to oppose the annexation of Adrianople by Bulgaria, and it was only after Russian military leaders had satisfied the Russian Foreign Office that the possession of Adrianople did not necessarily represent a threat to Constantinople that this opposition was withdrawn.[18]

It was in response to these Russian apprehensions that Great Britain proposed informally in November, 1912, the internationalization and neutralization of Constantinople, but the suggestion was received unfavorably both by Russia and France. Upon inquiry by France as to Russia's attitude, Sazonow stated, in December, 1912, Russia's desire to modify the régime of the Straits along the lines proposed by Izvolski in 1908, but indicated that Russia would not at present take the initiative.[19]

Indeed during the peace negotiations between the Balkan

[18] Turkey reoccupied Adrianople during the second Balkan war and succeeded in retaining it under Turkish sovereignty.

[19] See *Documents diplomatiques français (1871–1914)*, 3rd Ser. (1912–1914), Vol. 4, Nos. 364, 373, 559, 617; *British Documents*, Vol. IX, Pt. II, No. 143, p. 108; see also *Un livre Noir*, Vols. I and II, *passim*. Concerning France's attitude toward the Straits question during the Balkan wars see Poincaré, *op. cit.*, Vol. II, Chap. XII.

allies and Turkey which began at London in December, 1912, and lasted intermittently until the signature of the Treaty of London on May 30, 1913, the question of the Straits was never raised, although it doubtless influenced Russia's attitude. The restraint which Russia sought to impose on her Balkan protégées and her occasional espousals of Turkey's case were motivated not by any change of heart but by the desire to preserve Turkey sufficiently intact to keep Constantinople and the Straits until Russia was better prepared, diplomatically and militarily, to take them over. It was fear for the security of the Straits that led Russia to insist on leaving the strategic islands near the Dardanelles (Imbros, Tenedos, Samothrace and Lemnos) under Turkish sovereignty and to consent, finally, to their annexation by Greece only under the condition that they would be neutralized.[20]

Although the question of the Straits remained in the background during the Balkan wars, the policies of the Powers indicated their attitude toward the problem. Great Britain, in proposing internationalization of Constantinople, had showed her preference for such a solution as that urged by Russia during the Anglo-Russian negotiations in 1907 and during the Bosnian crisis in 1908. France does not seem to have been eager to give Russia a free hand. On the other hand, Russia apparently regarded the safeguarding of her interests in the Straits as paramount to any other consideration, even at the price of Bulgaria's defection from the

---

[20] The fate of these islands in the Aegean Sea was left to the determination of the Great Powers. After several months of wrangling, a decision was finally reached in February, 1914, leaving to Turkey only Imbros, Tenedos and Castellorizo. Not until the Treaty of Lausanne of July 24, 1923, did Turkey renounce sovereignty over the other islands in favor of Greece.

united front which Russia had been patiently trying to build up in the Balkans in years past.[21] While this policy postponed temporarily the complete liquidation of European Turkey, the outcome of the Balkan wars—both the change in the territorial *status quo* and the shift in the balance of power—accentuated the clash of interests centered around the Straits.

THE LIMAN VON SANDERS INCIDENT

No sooner was peace reestablished in the Balkans than the question of the Straits was raised in an acute form in consequence of the appointment of a German general, Herr Liman von Sanders, charged with the reorganization of the Turkish army, as commander of a Turkish army corps stationed at Constantinople.[22] The implications of German control of military forces in Constantinople were fully realized by the Entente Powers in general and by Russia in particular, where the news of Sanders' mission was received with alarm. Although the Turkish army had had German instructors since the end of the nineteenth century when Germany had begun to take an interest in Turkey, it seemed

[21] The opposition of Russia to the consummation of Bulgaria's victory by the occupation of Constantinople, her lukewarm attitude during the London Peace negotiations and during the third Balkan war in the summer of 1913, brought to an abrupt end the friendly devotion which the Bulgarians had felt ever since 1878 toward Russia. From this time on, Bulgaria definitely moved closer to the Central Powers.

[22] For the background and repercussions on the Sanders incident, consult *Die Grosse Politik*, Vol. 38, Chap. 290, pp. 191ff.; *British Documents*, Vol. X, Pt. I, Chap. 87, pp. 338ff.; *Documents diplomatiques français (1871–1914)*, 3rd Ser. (1912–1914), Vol. VIII, *passim*. For an excellent historical narrative, see R. J. Kerner, "The Mission of Liman von Sanders," *Slavonic Review*, Vol. 6, pp. 12ff., 244ff., 543ff.; Vol. 7, pp. 90ff. See also Taube, *op. cit.*, pp. 309ff.; Sazonow, *Fateful Years* (London, 1928), pp. 117–124.

to the Entente Powers that there was a vital difference between the rôle played by a host of German officers led by General von der Goltz, training the Turkish army, and the mission of Liman von Sanders who, with headquarters in the Turkish capital, appeared to dispose of far greater powers and influence. Russia, being most immediately concerned, made strong representations to Germany immediately after the nature of Sanders' functions became known in the fall of 1913, but without any success. For not only was Germany eager to tighten her hold on Turkey, but a point of German prestige was also involved: it had been a German-trained Turkish army which was defeated by the Balkan allies. Finding Germany intransigent, Sazonow sought to obtain the joint intervention of the Entente in Constantinople, but found both England and France rather reluctant to make a European issue out of the incident.[23] After several weeks during which the incident threatened to develop into a first-class crisis, Germany suddenly gave way: Liman von Sanders was promoted to a higher rank, as Inspector General, and he was thus automatically relieved of the more modest but real army post of corps commander.

The incident served to focus Russia's attention more than ever on the Straits. Already at the beginning of December, 1913, Sazonow had submitted a memorandum to the Czar, analyzing Russian policy in the Straits and asking for a conference of the Russian leaders concerned to examine the questions raised.[24] Sazonow's thesis as developed in the

[23] England particularly was in an embarrassing position since a British naval officer, Admiral Limpus, was commander of the Turkish navy with headquarters also in Constantinople, technically in the position of Liman von Sanders with respect to the Turkish army.

[24] For text, see *Un livre noir*, Vol. II, pp. 363ff.; for a good summary, see Mandelstam, *op. cit.*, pp. 734–38.

memorandum was, briefly, that Russia could not allow any Power other than Turkey—which was neither too strong nor too weak—to control the Straits; consequently, Russia must herself take possession of the Straits, should Turkey disintegrate. The conference decided that occupation of the Straits by Russia was impossible except in the case of a general European war and that at the moment Russian military preparations for such an expedition were wholly inadequate. Another report of Sazonow, dealing more directly with the Russo-German controversy over the Liman von Sanders mission, was discussed by key-members of the Government on January 13, 1914—a day before Germany liquidated the incident, in the manner above related. After examining the situation, the consensus of opinion was that Russia ought not to adopt measures likely to lead to war, unless the active participation of France and England could be secured—a question to which Sazonow did not have an affirmative reply.[25] His earlier report was discussed at a special conference on February 21, 1914, where the inadequacy of Russia's military preparedness was frankly acknowledged and plans were laid for building up the military and naval machine.[26]

[25] For a summary of Sazonow's report, see Mandelstam, op. cit., pp. 748–50; for the records of the conference of Jan. 13, 1914, see Stieve, op. cit., pp. 219ff. See also the illuminating ex post facto explanations of Count Kokovtzov, who as Prime Minister presided over this conference, op. cit., pp. 384ff. Cf. Florinsky, "Russia and Constantinople: Count Kokovtzov's Evidence," Foreign Affairs, Vol. 8 (1930), pp. 135ff.

[26] For the records of this special conference, see Stieve, op. cit., pp. 230ff. See also Sazonow, op. cit., pp. 125–127.

X

THE WORLD WAR

TURKEY'S NEUTRALITY

For nearly two months after the outbreak of the World War, Turkey was technically neutral. In fact, she committed herself to the Central Powers as early as August 2, 1914, by concluding a secret alliance with Germany. Searching for the motives of this step, many students have reached the conclusion that Turkey was forced by Germany, much against her will, to line up with the Central Powers. Yet it should be remembered that Germany's interests, as evidenced in the Bagdad railway, offered economic advantages to Turkey by opening up the hinterland of Anatolia, and at the same time helped to check the constant Russian threat to the control of the Straits. Although Turkey was undoubtedly subject to pressure by the presence of the mission of General Liman von Sanders and the influence Germany exercised through control of the Turkish army, it may be suggested that Turkey, faced with a choice between two evils, may have been less fearful of Germany than of her traditional antagonist, Russia. German influence could perhaps have been counterbalanced by Great Britain. But, as was pointed out before, British-Turkish relations had cooled perceptibly after the occupa-

tion of Cyprus and Egypt following the Russo-Turkish war
of 1877–78; whatever may have remained of the old friendship was relegated to the background by the resentment felt
in Turkey against Great Britain for sequestering, on the eve
of the war, two warships built for Turkey in English navy
yards. These ships would have given Turkey naval equality
with Greece and superiority over Russia's Black Sea fleet.

Turkey's ostensible neutrality was badly compromised
on August 10, 1914, when two German warships, the
Goeben and the *Breslau*, passed through the Dardanelles in
violation of the Straits Convention of July 13, 1841, reaffirmed by the treaties of 1856 and 1871, and anchored in
the port of Constantinople. Apart from the fact that passage through the Straits was in itself a breach of a treaty,
these ships should have been requested, under international
law, to leave within twenty-four hours; if the request were
not complied with, Turkey, as a neutral state, should have
interned the ships with their crews for the duration of the
war.[1] The German warships, however, remained in Constantinople and when the Allies protested, Turkey pur-

---

[1] Turkey was a signatory to the XIII Hague Convention of 1907 concerning the Rights and Duties of Neutral Powers in Naval War. Art. 12
of this Convention provides: "In the absence of special provisions to
the contrary in the legislation of a neutral Power, belligerent warships
are not permitted to remain in the ports, roadsteads, or territorial waters
of the said Power for more than twenty-four hours, except in the cases
covered in this Convention" (i.e., damage or stress of weather). Art. 24
provides: "If, notwithstanding the notification of the neutral Power, a
belligerent ship of war does not leave a port where it is not entitled to
remain, the neutral Power is entitled to take such measures as it considers necessary to render the ship incapable of taking the sea during
the war. . . . When a belligerent ship is detained by a neutral Power,
the officers and crew are likewise detained. . . ." Text in 36 U. S.
Statutes at Large, p. 2415; Malloy, *Treaties between the United States
and Other Powers*, Vol. 2, p. 2352; *British and Foreign State Papers*,
Vol. 100, p. 448.

chased the vessels from Germany for the Turkish navy. The transaction was blatantly fictitious; although the ships were rebaptized and recommissioned, they remained under the command of German naval officers and, in fact, Germany thus acquired control of the Straits. The Allies, not desiring to engage in open hostilities with Turkey, contented themselves with protests and warnings.

Another incident, far more serious in its consequences, occurred at the end of September. A Turkish warship was halted by a British destroyer just outside the Dardanelles and was forced to return. On the following day, September 27, 1914, Turkey closed the Straits and, while technically still neutral, cut a vital line of communication between the Western Allies and Russia.

A month later, on October 28, the Turkish fleet, now under German command and including the rebaptized *Breslau* and *Goeben*, ostensibly on manoeuvres in the Black Sea, attacked without a declaration of war units of the Russian fleet and bombarded a number of Russian ports. Russia replied on November 4 by declaring war on Turkey, and the other Allies followed suit. The Straits remained closed for the whole duration of the World War.[2]

The entry of Turkey into the war on the side of the Central Powers was doubtless one of the most significant events in the history of that conflict. It is generally believed that it prolonged the duration of the war; by cutting Russia off from the Western Allies, it put insurmountable obstacles in the way of provisioning the Russian army and thus reduced

[2] See Misc. No. 13 (1914) Cmd. 7628 and No. 14 (1914) Cmd. 7716. Correspondence respecting events leading to the rupture of relations with Turkey. Russia, Ministry for Foreign Affairs, *Recueil de documents diplomatiques, Négotiations ayant précédé la guerre avec la Turquie* (Petrograd, 1915).

the effectiveness of Russia's participation in the war; [2a] and it contributed, indirectly, by making Russia's defeat by the Central Powers possible, to the Bolshevik revolution. But these were consequences for the future. The immediate consequence of Turkey's conduct and action was to make the solution of the Straits question foremost among Russia's war aims and one of the decisive considerations of Russian policy until the advent of the Bolshevik régime.

The Secret Understandings Between the Allies Concerning the Straits

Russia did not formulate a definite policy regarding the solution of the Straits question until the campaign against the Dardanelles, early in 1915, projected the possibility of the occupation of Constantinople by the British and the French.[3] To incidental inquiries in London and Paris, Russia received more or less definite assurances that her Western Allies would agree to some solution conformable to Russian interests, contingent upon Germany's defeat.[4]

[2a] Concerning the economic consequences of the closure of the Straits, see Nolde, *Russia and the Economic War* (New Haven, Conn., 1928), pp. 38ff. [Carnegie Economic and Social History of the World War, Russian Series] *Cf.* Buchanan, *op. cit.*, Vol. I, pp. 223ff.

[3] The proclamation of the Czar, issued on October 31, 1914, following the Turkish attack on the Russian coast, vaguely referred to the expectation that the action of Turkey opened the path "towards the solution of the historic problem which our ancestors have bequeathed to us on the shores of the Black Sea." Paléologue, *An Ambassador's Memoirs*, Vol. I, p. 178. In a conversation with Paléologue, the French Ambassador at St. Petersburg, a few days after the war with Turkey, Sazonow indicated that whatever punishment he thought to impose on Turkey, he did not contemplate the annexation of Constantinople. *Ibid.* At the end of November, 1914, the Czar, in conversation with Paléologue, suggested the neutralization of Constantinople under international control. *Ibid.*, p. 192.

[4] See the reports of Count Benckendorff, Russian Ambassador at London, to Sazonow, dated November 9, 1914, concerning his conversa-

But when the plan of a campaign against the Dardanelles emerged, Russia was no longer satisfied with these vague promises. The idea of such a campaign was suggested by Russia herself early in January, 1915. Hard pressed by the Turks on the Caucasian front, an attack on the Dardanelles was suggested as a means to distract the attention of the Turks. But in the hands of British naval and military experts, the plan as evolved contemplated not a mere demonstration to relieve Turkish pressure on one of Russia's fronts, but occupation of the Straits and the reestablishment of the line of communication between the Western Allies and Russia. The plan in this form was received with ill-concealed suspicion by many in Russia, although both the British and the French urged and expected the cooperation of Russian naval and military forces, which cooperation the Russians felt unable to offer.[4a] This suspicion was heightened when England proposed to enlist the active participation of Greece. Fearful of Greek ambitions and apprehensive of the question of prestige involved in Greek troops entering Constantinople while the Russians would be ab-

___

tion with Sir Edward Grey, *Constantinople et les Détroits*, Vol. I, No. XVIII, p. 144; dated Nov. 13, concerning his conversation with King George V, *ibid.*, No. XXI, p. 148; the memorandum of the British Embassy at St. Petersburg to Sazonow, dated November 14, *ibid.*, No. XXIII, p. 151. The French Government assured Russia even before Turkey's entry into the war of its support of Russian claims in the Straits; see Izvolski's report to Sazonow, dated October 13, 1914, Stieve, *op. cit.*, p. 247.

[4a] Some Russian military leaders apparently doubted the possibility, from the military point of view, of Russia's then realizing her historic ambition in the Straits. See the review of correspondence between Sazonow and Prince Kudashev, the representative of the Russian Foreign Office at Army headquarters in Florinsky, "A Page of Diplomatic History: Russian Military Leaders and the Problem of Constantinople during the War," *Political Science Quarterly*, Vol. 44, pp. 108ff. (1929).

sent, Sazonow categorically vetoed this plan.[5] Russia was opposed, for the same reason, to the efforts to bring Italy into the war on the side of the Allies.[6] The campaign against the Dardanelles began on February 19, 1915, and the fear that, once the Straits were occupied by the British and the French, Russia would be left high and dry, impelled Sazonow to force a definite and unequivocal commitment from Russia's allies.[7]

On March 4, 1915, Mr. Sazonow presented a memorandum to the British and French ambassadors at St. Petersburg in which, guaranteeing respect for the interests of England and France, the Western Allies were requested to consent to the outright annexation by Russia of Constantinople, the European coast of the Bosphorus, the Sea of Marmora with its islands and the Dardanelles, together with the islands of Imbros and Tenedos, Southern Thrace up to the Enos-Midia line, and a small strip of the Asiatic shores along the Ismid peninsula.[8]

[5] Concerning Russia's attitude toward Greek participation in the operations against the Straits, see *Constantinople et les Détroits*, Vol. II, Nos. 94–115, pp. 97–119.

[6] *Ibid.*, Vol. I, Nos. CVIII–CXXV, pp. 255–288.

[7] Viscount Grey summed up the Russian point of view as follows: "It had always been British policy to keep Russia out of Constantinople and the Straits; we fought for that object in the Crimean war of the fifties, and it was our main policy under Beaconsfield in the seventies of the nineteenth century; of course it was our policy still. Britain was now going to occupy Constantinople in order that when Britain and France had been enabled, by Russia's help, to win the war, Russia should not have Constantinople at the peace." *Twenty-Five Years*, Vol. II, p. 187.

[8] For the text of Sazonow's memorandum, see *Constantinople et les Détroits*, Vol. I, No. XLIX, p. 175; *Un livre noir*, Vol. III, p. 122. On March 1, Sazonow called the attention of the British and French ambassadors to the general excitement of the Russian public over the question of Constantinople. He said that the whole country demanded a "radical solution"; that the hour for plain speaking had come, and

Under the pressure of war conditions and in view of the
necessity of keeping Russia in line, there was not much
that England and France could do but assent to Russia's demands which Sazonow insisted should be kept an absolute
secret, lest knowledge thereof alienate from the Allies some
neutral countries concerned—particularly Rumania and Bulgaria. Their consent was forthcoming—curiously the British satisfied Russia before France did. But the diplomatic
exchanges show clearly that the boldness of Sazonow's
claims was somewhat of a shock both to Sir Edward Grey
and to Delcassé, the French Foreign Minister, and that
neither Great Britain nor France acquiesced with any great
enthusiasm in Russia's "radical solution" of the Straits question. The correspondence between Great Britain, France,
Russia and, later, Italy also show that this acquiescence was
at a price—namely the consent of Russia to the satisfaction
of British, French and Italian claims and the recognition by
her of their spheres of interest in the Near East, all at the
expense of the Ottoman Empire. Thus, it was Russia's demand for Constantinople and the Straits which set the
stage for spoils and the pyramid of conflicting secret
treaties which were later to embarrass the Allies and to
create new sources of friction, even though the secret treaty

---

England and France should say openly that they agreed to the annexation of Constantinople by Russia when the day for peace arrived.
Paléologue, *op. cit.*, Vol. I, p. 295. Two days later the Czar himself
spoke to Paléologue in a similar vein. He said that the Russian people
must be rewarded for the terrible sacrifices of the war with the realization of their time-honored ambition. Therefore, he had made up his
mind to adopt the radical solution and incorporate Constantinople and
Southern Thrace into the Russian Empire. The Czar added that he was
counting on the French Government's help to settle any misunder-
standings which might arise in this respect with England. *Ibid.*, pp. 297–
98.

relating to the Straits was to lapse because of Russia's desertion of the Allies.[9]

Finally, it appears from the records that the confidence between the Allies was not too great. Great Britain reversed a century-old policy very unwillingly and France, who because of her alliance was much closer to Russia than any of the Allied Powers, was even more reluctant than England to concede what Paris regarded as the somewhat exorbitant claims of Russia. Italy was not even informed of the understanding when she joined the Allies; when the matter could no longer be kept secret from her, she also gave her consent reluctantly—and for a price.[10]

[9] The important documents relating to the secret agreements conceding Constantinople and the Straits are printed in *Constantinople et les Détroits*, Vol. I. The British reply constituting acceptance of Russia's demand is dated March 12, 1915, *op. cit.*, No. LXXVII, p. 205; the French acceptance was forthcoming only after some wrangling on April 10, 1915, *ibid.*, No. XCIX, p. 232. These arrangements were completed by assurances given to Russia by the British and French Governments, on April 22 and 23, 1915, respectively, that the Allied commitments to Italy in no way affected understandings already arrived at between the three governments. *Ibid.*, Nos. CXXXI and CXXXII, pp. 284–85. Concerning French reaction to Russian claims to the Straits see Poincaré, *op. cit.*, Vol. VI, Chap. III, pp. 86ff. For Sazonow's own account of the negotiations with the Allies see his *Fateful Years*, pp. 245ff.

[10] The agreement concerning the Straits was communicated to Italy only in October, 1916. In a memorandum of November 6, 1916, the Italian Ambassador at St. Petersburg advised Russia that Italy would assent to the understanding relating to Constantinople and the Straits if she could share equally the privileges secured in that region for France and Great Britain and if she could realize her aspirations in the Near East. An exchange of notes between the Russian Ambassador at Rome and the Italian Foreign Office on December 2, 1916, records Italy's acquiescence in the annexation of Constantinople and the Straits by Russia. See *Constantinople et les Détroits*, Vol. I, Nos. CLIII, p. 305, CLVII, p. 309, CLXV, p. 344 and CLXVI, p. 345.

Bolshevik Russia Renounces Claims to the Straits

While the provisional Russian government under Prince Lwow, which assumed power after the first revolution in March, 1917, intended to continue fighting in the Allied camp, its intention to maintain Russian claims under the secret treaties was disavowed by the Bolshevik party which, on this issue, forced the resignation of Foreign Minister Miliukow and proclaimed its opposition to annexation. When the Bolsheviks gained control in the fall of 1917, they promptly published and denounced the secret treaties with the Allies, renouncing, specifically, all claims to Constantinople and the Straits which, they declared, ought to remain under Turkish sovereignty. The beginning of separate peace negotiations with the Central Powers at the end of 1917 gave the Allies the signal to proclaim the lapse of the secret agreements with Russia. The question of the Straits once more emerged, awaiting solution; and there is no evidence showing that either Great Britain, France or Italy were disturbed by Russia's abandonment of her claims to the Straits, however much they may have regretted Russia's withdrawal from the war.[11]

Although the separate peace treaty between the Central Powers and Soviet Russia, concluded at Brest-Litovsk on March 3, 1918, fell far short of the program of the Bolsheviks for a peace based on no annexations and no indemnities, the action of Russia in voluntarily renouncing any conquest has a very important influence on post-war Russo-Turkish

[11] For the attitude of the provisional government and of the Bolsheviks toward the secret treaties and the Straits question, see *Constantinople et les Détroits*, Vol. I, Nos. CCCI–CCCLXIV, pp. 458–526; Howard, *The Partition of Turkey*, pp. 194–196, 198–200.

relations. Coupled with the assistance which the Soviet gave to Turkey in the Greco-Turkish war during 1919–1922, it laid the foundation for cooperation between the two countries and for friendlier feeling than had existed between these two states at any time for a century.

XI

THE PEACE SETTLEMENT

THE TREATY OF SÉVRES AND THE GRECO-TURKISH WAR

HAVING been freed from commitments to Russia, the Allies were confronted with the question of what to do with the Straits. Great Britain and the United States, which had now become a belligerent, were quick to formulate a program envisaging complete freedom of passage through the Straits under international control. Mr. Lloyd George, speaking on January 5, 1918, before the Trade Unions Congress on the war aims of the Allies, denied that the Allies intended to take the Turkish capital but insisted on the necessity of neutralizing and internationalizing the Straits. On January 8, President Wilson published the Fourteen Points, Point XII declaring that "the Dardanelles should be permanently opened as a free passage to the ships and commerce of all nations under international guarantees." [1]

The Allied victory made possible, for the time being at least, the realization of this program. The armistice of Mudros, signed on October 30, 1918, provided for the opening of the Straits and Allied occupation of Con-

---

[1] See also Mr. Lansing's memorandum of September 21, 1918, for the American Peace Commissioners in his book, *The Peace Negotiations* (Boston, 1921), pp. 192ff.

stantinople as well as of all strategic points along the Dardanelles and the Bosphorus.[2] In fact, this occupation was carried out largely by British forces which remained in control of the Straits until the conclusion of the Treaty of Lausanne in July, 1923. Turkey seemed completely at the mercy of the Allies. The plan to give the United States a mandate over Constantinople and the Straits was frustrated by President Wilson's refusal,[3] while an outright annexation or even a mandate by any of the European Allies was out of the question in view of the jealousies between Great Britain, France and Italy (which were responsible, indirectly, for the resumption of hostilities between Greece and Turkey) concerning their Near Eastern possessions and spheres of interest. Inability to compose their differences induced the Allies to leave Turkey nominally sovereign over Constantinople and to propose an ostensibly international control over the demilitarized Straits.

The Treaty of Sèvres of August 10, 1920,[4] between the Allies and Turkey was never ratified, but its stipulations are of interest since they served as a model for the final settlement of the Straits question in the convention annexed to the Treaty of Lausanne three years later. Under the Treaty of Sèvres, Constantinople was left to Turkey, subject to any modification of its status by the Allies, should Turkey fail to observe her treaty obligations. Navigation in the Straits was to be open both in peace and in war to

---

[2] For the text of the armistice, see *Livre rouge* (Turkish Red Book, 1925), No. 1; Temperley, *A History of the Peace Conference of Paris*, Vol. I, pp. 495-97.

[3] Temperley, *op. cit.*, Vol. VI, pp. 26-29; Howard, *op. cit.*, pp. 231ff.

[4] For the text of the treaty, see *British Treaty Series* No. 11 (1920), Cmd. 964. The provisions relating to the Straits are reprinted in Appendix No. 1, p. 137.

the merchant vessels and warships, including aircraft, of all nations. Except for action undertaken pursuant to a decision of the League of Nations, no act of hostility could be committed in the Straits and the area could not be blockaded. A commission was to be set up composed of the Principal Allied and Associated Powers, each of them having two votes, Greece and Rumania; Russia, Bulgaria and Turkey were to be given seats on the commission upon their admission to the League of Nations. The commission was invested with broad powers, to be exercised wholly independently of the local authorities, and could invoke the assistance of the troops which the treaty authorized the Allies to maintain in the region, in case of interference with freedom of passage, which was to be insured by the demolition of all fortifications within the Straits.

However, the Government at Constantinople which had been forced to sign the Treaty of Sèvres was no longer in control of Turkey. The landing of Greek troops in Smyrna on May 14, 1919, with the permission of Great Britain and France—a permission granted partly in order to forestall Italy in the Near East—signified not only the renewal of hostilities between Turkey and Greece in Asia Minor but also a turning point in Turkish history. From the resistance against Greek invasion, there developed the nationalist movement and, ultimately, a reborn Turkey sufficiently strong to challenge successfully the authority of the Allies and to overthrow the ignominious peace settlement which the Allies intended to impose on the "sick man of Europe."

While the Greco-Turkish war was fought largely in Asiatic Turkey and except in its later phase did not threaten the Allied position in the Straits, its consequences had a decided effect on the balance of power in the Eastern Mediterranean. Allied intervention in Russia, made possible through the control of the Straits, and Allied support of the Greek adventure inevitably brought the Soviet and Nationalist Turkey together. Opposition to a common enemy—the Western Allies—facilitated a compromise over Armenia which constituted the main cause of contention between Russia and Turkey, and on March 16, 1921, a treaty signed at Moscow laid the foundations for friendly relations and cooperation between the two countries which, despite occasional setbacks and, later, decreasing cordiality, lasted until the fall of 1939. In this treaty Russia recognized the integrity of Turkey as defined by the National Pact framed in January, 1920, and adopted by the Turkish Grand National Assembly at Angora on April 23, 1920;[5] and voluntarily renounced in Turkey's favor the Trans-Caucasian territories which Russia acquired in the Russo-Turkish war of 1877–78 (with the exception of Batum and a small strip of territory around that port).[6]

Turkey further consolidated her position by treaties concluded with other states of the Soviet Union [7] and Russia,

[5] For text, see Temperley, *op. cit.*, Vol. VI, p. 605.

[6] For the text of the treaty of March 16, 1921, see *British and Foreign State Papers*, Vol. 118, p. 990; Martens, *Nouveau recueil général des traités* (3rd Ser.), Vol. 16, pp. 37ff.; see also Toynbee, *Survey of International Affairs*, 1920–1923, pp. 370–74. Russia was forced to cede these territories to Turkey in the treaty of Brest-Litovsk of March 3, 1918. Text in *British and Foreign State Papers*, Vol. 123, pp. 740ff. But the victory of the Allies freed Russia from the obligations imposed on her by the Central Powers, and her voluntary reaffirmation of this cession three years later was an important factor in creating a friendly attitude toward Soviet Russia in Turkey.

[7] Treaty of Kars with the Caucasian states, October 13, 1921. Martens, *Nouveau recueil général des traités* (3rd Ser.), Vol. 30, pp. 17ff. Treaty of Friendship with Ukrainian Soviet, January 21, 1922. *British and Foreign State Papers*, Vol. 120, p. 453.

emerging from the desperate struggles with domestic revolution and foreign intervention, gave effective assistance in
the form of arms and money to Turkey in her war against
Greece.

No less important for Turkey's rehabilitation was the
conclusion of separate agreements between the Angora
Government on the one hand and France and Italy on the
other.[8] France, who was suspicious of, and Italy, decidedly
hostile to, British aspirations in the Near East and fearful
of England's preponderant position in that region because
of her naval supremacy, were quick to abandon the Allied
front at the first indication that the Greek expedition might
end in a failure, and sought to insure their own interest
by dealing separately with the Kemalist government. Thus
they left Great Britain virtually the sole opponent of
Turkey. Thanks to the active assistance of Soviet Russia,
to the shrewd policy of the Turkish leadership in consoli-
dating the country's diplomatic position and to the fine
spirit of the revitalized Turkish army, the Greco-Turkish
war ended in the disastrous defeat of Greece. In the last
phase of the war, the march of the victorious Turkish
armies threatened to bring about an open armed conflict
with Great Britain.

It was after several months of stalemate that the Turkish
army launched into a large scale offensive along the
Sakaria on August 18, 1922. Within three weeks, the

---

[8] Treaty of March 12, 1921, between Turkey and Italy concerning
the economic exploitation of Southern Anatolia. Martens, *Nouveau
recueil général de traités* (3rd Ser.), Vol. 13, pp. 335ff. Treaty of
October 21, 1921, between France and Turkey. *League of Nations
Treaty Series*, Vol. 54, p. 177. *British and Foreign State Papers*, Vol. 114,
p. 771; concerning the controversy between Great Britain and France
relating to this agreement, see *ibid.*, pp. 293ff.

Greek army was for practical purposes non-existent; on September 9, Smyrna was in Turkish hands and there were indications that the Turks were contemplating crossing the Straits and driving the Greeks out of Eastern Thrace. Although each of the Allies had resident commissioners in Constantinople and they jointly advised the Turkish command that no violation of the demilitarized zone would be permitted, England alone seems to have been concerned about the fate of the Straits. British troops were rushed to reinforce the defenses of Constantinople against possible attack and to prevent the Turks from regaining control over the Straits. An appeal by Great Britain first to France and Italy and later to the Dominions, Yugoslavia, Rumania and Greece for armed assistance in the defense of the Straits found unenthusiastic reception; in fact, the French and Italian governments, annoyed and deeply suspicious of the motives of Great Britain's policy, replied a few days later by recalling their troops stationed in Chanak and other strategic points, leaving it to the British to take care of themselves and the Straits as best they could.[9]

Fortunately, an armed conflict was avoided. The Allies proposed an armistice preliminary to an international conference to settle the whole Eastern question. Turkey accepted the proposal at the end of September and expressed willingness not to move against the neutral zone of Chanak and the Straits under certain conditions. An energetic warning by the British commander at Chanak not to threaten British positions followed, and negotiations for the armistice continued without any incident. The armistice, providing for the withdrawal of the Greek army behind

[9] Temperley, *op. cit.*, Vol. VI, p. 38; Howard, *op. cit.*, pp. 268–72.

the Maritza River, temporary Allied occupation of the evacuated zone and the establishment of neutral zones, was signed at Mudania on October 11, 1922.[10]

The signing of the armistice ended the war in the Near East; it also ended a not very laudable chapter in British foreign policy, the failure of which was to no small extent the reason for the resignation of Mr. Lloyd George a week later.

THE STRAITS QUESTION AT THE LAUSANNE CONFERENCE

At the Conferénce of Lausanne which opened on November 20, 1922, the question of the Straits played a prominent part. Inasmuch as Turkey had accepted at an early stage of the negotiations the principle of freedom of passage, the chief antagonists were once more Great Britain and Russia. But the historic position of the two countries on this issue was reversed.

Great Britain, opposed for a century to opening the Straits to warships, now advocated freedom of passage, while Russia, whose fondest ambition under the Czars had been to secure egress to the Mediterranean, now under a communist government sought to close the Straits altogether. The reversal of position, however, was not wholly surprising. Control and closure of the Straits by Turkey during the World War proved to be a serious handicap for the Allies in the prosecution of the war, and Great Britain at least—even if France and Italy did not—now regarded it an advantage to be able to hold Soviet Russia in check by keeping the Straits open to warships under international

[10] Text in Giannini, *I Documenti diplomatici della pace orientale* (Roma, 1922), pp. 251-53.

control, even though some concessions had to be made to the Turks on the extent and form of this control for the security of Constantinople as well as for Turkish prestige. It should also be remembered that what England had opposed was not the opening of the Straits generally but a one-sided arrangement opening them to Russian or other Black Sea Powers only without reciprocal permission of ingress from the Mediterranean into the Black Sea. In reciprocal freedom for non-riverain Powers to enter the Black Sea, England had nothing to fear; on the contrary, naval superiority gave her an advantageous position over Black Sea Powers and particularly Russia, as Allied intervention in Russia, possible only through the opening of the Straits, clearly demonstrated. Russia, on the other hand, found the free passage of Allied warships and troop transports into the Black Sea and the assistance thus given to the enemies of the Bolshevik revolution most disagreeable and, in view of the utter inadequacy of her disorganized Black Sea fleet and the slender hope of building a strong naval force, her position exceedingly vulnerable. The Soviet delegate at Lausanne therefore fought for the closure of the Straits to warships of all nations at all times. The positions taken by Imperial Russia and the Soviet are not irreconcilable if we remember that Prince Gortchakoff, Izvolski and Sazonow preferred to leave the régime of the Straits unaltered rather than open both for egress and for ingress.[11]

Despite the bitter oppositon of Tchicherin, who represented Soviet Russia in the first phase of the Lausanne Con-

---

[11] For the conflicting views of Great Britain and Soviet Russia concerning the régime of the Straits, see the minutes of the meetings of the First Commission in *Lausanne Conference on Near Eastern Affairs 1922–23*. Cmd. 1814 (1923).

ference, the Straits Convention of 1923, annexed to the Lausanne treaty, was based on the principle of freedom of passage advocated by Great Britain. Had the Turkish delegates ranged themselves with the Soviet, the outcome might have been different. Curiously, the Turks, although virtually allied with the Soviet and indebted for its assistance in the war with Greece, did not succumb to the temptation which the solution proposed by Tchicherin—complete Turkish sovereignty over the Straits—doubtless offered. Whether Turkey's aloofness from the British-Russian controversy was due to the cautious desire of Turkish statesmen not to get into too close an association with the Soviet, or to the success of the British policy which now definitely sought to separate Turkey from Russia, is impossible to say; perhaps it was a combination of both. Turkey's attitude seems realistic enough considering that she no longer needed to seek active assistance from Russia; and having again installed themselves at Constantinople, the Turks, remembering her time-honored ambitions in that region, may have been wary of putting too much reliance on Russia.

XII

THE STRAITS CONVENTION OF 1923

The Régime Under the Lausanne Convention

In Art. 23 of the Treaty of Lausanne, signed on July 24, 1923, by the representatives of the British Empire, France, Italy, Japan, Greece, Rumania, Yugoslavia and Turkey, the signatories agreed

"to recognize and declare the principle of freedom of transit and of navigation, by sea and by air, in time of peace as in time of war, in the strait of the Dardanelles, the Sea of Marmora and the Bosphorus, as prescribed in the separate Convention signed this day, regarding the régime of the Straits." [1]

The "Convention relating to the Straits" signed the same day reiterated, in Art. 1, the principle of freedom declared in Art. 23 of the Lausanne treaty and an annex to Art. 2 laid down detailed rules to govern the passage of merchant vessels, warships and aircraft, both civil and military, through the Dardanelles, the Bosphorus and the Sea of Marmora, all of which were comprised under the general term of the "Straits." These rules called for full freedom of passage day and night for merchant vessels (including hospital

[1] For the text of the Lausanne treaty, see *British Treaty Series* No. 16 (1923). Cmd. 1929.

ships, yachts, fishing boats and civil aircraft) of all nations, irrespective of the nature of cargo, both in peace and in war, Turkey being neutral; in case of Turkish belligerency, Turkey was left free to exercise belligerent rights under international law; i.e., she could attack and capture enemy merchantmen and she could visit and search neutral merchant ships to prevent their giving assistance to her enemies by carrying contraband, troops or enemy nationals. With respect to warships (including auxiliary and troop ships, aircraft carriers and military aircraft), freedom of passage was provided without distinction of flag but no Power might send into the Black Sea a force larger than that of the most powerful fleet maintained in that sea by a littoral state at the time of passage. This limitation, introduced in the interest of the Black Sea Powers, was considerably weakened by the further proviso that each of the Powers might always send into the Black Sea three ships at most, none of which should exceed 10,000 tons. In other words, the door was left open for the sending into the Black Sea at all times of non-riparian naval forces superior to the Black Sea fleet. In time of war, Turkey being neutral, the same rules and limitations were applicable to neutral warships, but the limitations did not apply to belligerent warships to the detriment of their belligerent rights in the Black Sea. Such belligerent warships might not commit hostilities, or exercise the right of visit, search and capture in the Straits. Finally, in case of Turkish belligerency, freedom of passage was given to neutral warships only, and measures taken by Turkey to prevent passage of enemy forces were not to prejudice neutral rights; but neutral military aircraft might pass only at their own risk. Submarines must navigate in the Straits on the surface.

To insure freedom of passage, the Convention provided for the demilitarization of both the European and the Asiatic shores of the Bosphorus and the Dardanelles with the exception of the right of Turkey to maintain a garrison not exceeding 12,000 men, an arsenal and a naval base in Constantinople and subject to Turkey's right to transport her armed forces through the demilitarized zones. The islands in the Sea of Marmora and the Greek and Turkish islands in the Aegean Sea, commanding the entrance to the Straits (Samothrace, Lemnos, Imbros, Tenedos, and Rabbit Islands) were also demilitarized; Turkey and Greece, when belligerent, would be entitled to remilitarize these areas subject to the duty of notifying the signatories and of restoring the *status quo* at the end of the war. The freedom of passage was to be insured and supervised by the constitution of an International Straits Commission composed of one representative of each of the signatory powers (the United States also being entitled to a seat upon accession to the convention), under the permanent presidency of Turkey and functioning under the auspices of the League of Nations to which it was to make an annual report. To counterbalance the "unjustifiable danger" which the demilitarization of the Straits and of the contiguous zones might constitute to the military safety of Turkey and to safeguard the freedom of the Straits, the signatories, but particularly Great Britain, France, Italy and Japan, acting jointly, agreed to meet any threat to the freedom or security of the Straits by all the means that the Council of the League may decide for that purpose. This collective guarantee was declared to form an integral part of the provisions relating to the demilitarization and to the freedom of the Straits, without prejudice, however, to the rights and obligations of the signatories under the League Covenant.[2]

These were, then, the rules which governed navigation in the Straits from 1923 to 1936. The régime established by the Straits Convention represented a compromise between the interests of the Black Sea Powers—particularly those of Russia—seeking preferential treatment,[4] and the ambition of the Allies—particularly of Great Britain—seeking complete freedom. From the point of view of Turkey, it represented substantial improvement over the situation envisaged in the Treaty of Sèvres. While the Convention still imposed limitations on Turkey's freedom of action, the security of Constantinople was better safeguarded and the requirements of Turkish prestige were, for the time being, more or less adequately satisfied. The improvement in Turkey's military and diplomatic position in 1923 as compared with 1920 can be measured by the difference between the relevant provisions of the Sèvres treaty and the Straits Convention.[3]

FROM LAUSANNE TO MONTREUX

The régime established by the Convention of 1923 proved to be acceptable to most of the interested powers

[2] For the text of the Straits Convention of 1923, see Appendix No. 2, p. 142. It came into force upon the deposit of the required number of ratifications on August 6, 1924. Russia did not sign the Convention until August 14, 1923, and the Soviet Government subsequently indicated its disapproval by refusing to ratify it. Yugoslavia, because of a dispute with Turkey over the Ottoman Public Debt, did not sign.

[3] For an excellent analysis of the Straits Convention from the point of view of international law, see F. de Visscher, "Nouveau régime des détroits," *Revue de droit international et de legislation comparée*, Vol. 4 (3rd Ser.), pp. 537ff. (1923), Vol. 5, pp. 13ff. (1924). See also: Rougier, "La question des détroits et la Convention de Lausanne," *Revue général de droit international public*, Vol. 31, pp. 309ff. (1924).

and worked satisfactorily during the period of comparative calm which reigned in Europe for a decade following the Lausanne Conference. In such a period, freedom of passage was beneficial to international trade, and while demilitarization put the Straits and Turkey's security in that region at the mercy of any strong naval power, this shortcoming of the arrangement could be considered temporary in anticipation of general reduction of armaments and of further stabilization of peace. The country most dissatisfied with the arrangement was Soviet Russia which felt herself exposed and threatened. Failure of the Turkish representatives at the Lausanne Conference to support the Soviet point of view was not too well received in Moscow and might well have put an end to Russo-Turkish friendship. However, circumstances induced both countries to continue their friendly relations with each other. Despite the fact that each improved its relations with Western Europe, they were both still outside the "concert" of powers. Neither Turkey nor Russia was a member of the League of Nations. Turkey particularly did not wish to antagonize Russia because the Mosul question, unsolved by the Lausanne treaty, still barred genuine rapprochement with Great Britain. Moreover, Turkish diplomacy was sufficiently shrewd to appreciate the advantages which it might derive from Soviet diplomatic support whenever Turkey should deem it opportune to press for revision of the régime so distasteful to Russia and by no means satisfactory to Turkey. Russian diplomacy was equally astute in comprehending that a Turkey favorably inclined toward Moscow would be more likely to prevent exploitation of Russia's disadvantageous position in the Black Sea by powers antagonistic to the Soviets, and that Russia had every reason to refrain from conduct which would drive Turkey into the arms of the Western Allies.

Continued Russo-Turkish cooperation was demonstrated by the signature of a treaty of neutrality and non-aggression on December 17, 1925. In this treaty, Russia and Turkey agreed to maintain neutrality should one of the parties be attacked by a third power and to make no political or military alliance directed against the other signatory.[4]

It perhaps was not wholly an accident that the Russo-Turkish treaty was signed on the day following the decision of the League Council awarding Mosul to Great Britain, to the great disappointment of the Turks. Alarmed by the prospect of a Russo-Turkish combination, British diplomacy strove to liquidate the Mosul dispute and, since Turkey was somewhat reluctant to align herself irrevocably with Soviet Russia, a settlement satisfactory to both parties was quickly reached. A tripartite treaty between Great Britain, Turkey and Iraq, signed on June 5, 1926,[5] terminated a long period of strained British-Turkish relations which had caused Turkey's alignment with Germany before the World War and since with Soviet Russia. The door was thus opened to gradual rapprochement of Turkey with the Western European Powers—an opportunity of which Turkey availed herself with caution. The progress of this rapprochement was marked by the successive con-

[4] For the text of the treaty, see *League of Nations Treaty Series*, Vol. 157, p. 353; *British and Foreign State Papers*, Vol. 125, p. 1001.

[5] *British Treaty Series* No. 18 (1927). Cmd. 2912; *British and Foreign State Papers*, Vol. 123, p. 599; *League of Nations Treaty Series*, Vol. 64, p. 379.

clusion of treaties of friendship with Italy,[6] France[7] and Greece,[8] and the admission of Turkey into the League of Nations in 1932.[9] To the extent that Turkey improved her relations with the Western Powers, she became less dependent on Russia; nevertheless, she remained outwardly on the best terms with her northern neighbors almost up to the unsuccessful Moscow negotiations in the fall of 1939. In substance, however, Russo-Turkish relations began to cool, imperceptibly, from the late twenties on when the consolidation of Turkey's diplomatic position with respect to the Allies was more or less accomplished.[10]

Turkey's move for revision of the Straits Convention of 1923 was preceded by a series of events which profoundly altered the foundations upon which post-war Europe was erected. This fundamental change was brought about by a series of treaty repudiations, undeclared wars, the failure of the Disarmament and the World Economic conferences, the increasingly "dynamic" foreign policies of authoritarian governments and the consequent whittling away of the collective security system. For Turkey to raise the question of the Straits under such conditions was both logical and understandable. Both the time and the

[6] Treaty of Neutrality, Conciliation and Judicial Settlement, signed on May 30, 1928. *League of Nations Treaty Series,* Vol. 95, p. 185; *British and Foreign State Papers,* Vol. 129, p. 763.

[7] Treaty of Neutrality, Conciliation and Arbitration, signed on February 3, 1930. *British and Foreign State Papers,* Vol. 132, p. 777.

[8] Treaty of Neutrality, Conciliation, and Arbitration, signed on October 30, 1930. *League of Nations Treaty Series,* Vol. 125, p. 9; *British and Foreign State Papers,* Vol. 132, p. 814.

[9] *League of Nations Official Journal, Special Supplement No. 102.* Records of the Special Session of the Assembly, pp. 21-23. Eighth Plenary Meeting, July 18, 1932.

[10] See Toynbee, *Survey of International Affairs,* 1928, pp. 358-74, for a review of the gradual deterioration of Turko-Soviet relations from 1926 onward.

method chosen by Turkey were merely further evidences of the astuteness and perspicacity of Turkish statesmanship.

TURKEY REQUESTS REVISION OF THE STRAITS CONVENTION

In a note dated April 10, 1936, addressed to the signatories of the 1923 Convention, to Yugoslavia and the Secretary General of the League of Nations, the Turkish Government requested the convocation of a conference for the revision of the demilitarization clauses of the Straits Convention.[11] The request came at the height of the Italo-Abyssinian war, which was disturbing the *status quo* in the Eastern Mediterranean, and followed closely the remilitarization of the Rhineland by Germany's unilateral action. The replies to the Turkish move were immediate and favorable; the Great Powers, including Japan and with the sole exception of Italy, smarting under sanctions and at odds with the world at large, promptly accepted the idea of revision by conference and negotiation. There was hesitation only on the part of Turkey's allies in the Balkan Entente (especially Rumania) who, in the light of ostensible Russo-Turkish friendship, feared that a change

[11] For the text of the note, see *League of Nations Official Journal*, 1936, p. 504; *Documents on International Affairs*, 1936, pp. 645ff. The question of remilitarization of the Straits had been alluded to on several previous occasions but never formally pressed by the Turkish representatives. See the Disarmament Conference, *Minutes of the General Commission*, Vol. 2, pp. 481ff.; *League of Nations Official Journal*, 1935, p. 562 (Minutes of the 85th Session of the Council); *League of Nations Official Journal*, Special Supplement No. 138, Records of the Sixteenth Ordinary Session of the Assembly (1935), p. 76, Eighth Plenary Meeting, September 14, 1935. On all these occasions the Turkish allusions were received with polite but non-committal interest by the Western Powers. Turkey also indicated her desire to change the régime of the Straits at meetings of the Balkan Entente.

might adversely affect their interests and security in the Black Sea. Great Britain, anxious to strengthen her position in the Mediterranean, was more than ever eager to solidify her friendship with Turkey. France, now bound to Russia by an alliance, was no longer apprehensive of increased Soviet influence in the Near East. Soviet Russia, finally, never reconciled to the régime established at Lausanne, was exceedingly pleased with the prospect of eliminating the danger to which she felt herself exposed, especially since she believed that Turkey, once again master of the Straits, was and would remain a friend of Moscow.

The Conference met at Montreux on June 22, 1936. With the exception of Italy, all signatories of the Lausanne Convention were represented; Yugoslavia, which did not sign the 1923 Convention, also sent a delegate; and pursuant to the transformation of the British Empire into the British Commonwealth of Nations, the self-governing Dominions either sent representatives (Australia) or advised the Conference that they would accept its decisions. The draft convention submitted by the Turkish representatives went far beyond the indication in the Turkish note of April 10, 1936, as to her plan of revision; it proposed not merely a refortification of the Straits but was also intended to make Turkey absolute master over navigation, especially in time of war, and to establish a régime exceedingly favorable to Russia.

Once more it was Great Britain which objected to such a modification of the régime of the Straits and found herself, as at the Lausanne Conference, in sharp opposition to Soviet Russia, which was seeking, this time successfully, to reassert the familiar argument inherited from imperial days concerning her *sui generis* position in the Black Sea.

Again, as at Lausanne, the battle over the Straits was fought principally between the British and Soviet representatives. When the Conference reconvened at the beginning of July after a short adjournment, the British submitted their own draft which differed substantially in several respects from the proposals put forward by the Turks at the beginning of the Conference. The Montreux Convention, as finally adopted on July 20, 1936, represented a compromise between the Turkish and British drafts, arrived at after two weeks of debate between the British and Soviet delegations.[12]

[12] For the records of the Montreux Conference, see *Actes de la Conférence de Montreux* (Paris, 1936). For an analysis of the background of the position taken by the powers and a thoughtful survey of the process whereby the final text was agreed upon, see D. A. Routh, "The Montreux Convention Regarding the Régime of the Black Sea Straits," in *Survey of International Affairs*, 1936, pp. 584–651.

XIII

THE MONTREUX CONVENTION OF 1936

THE Convention signed on July 20, 1936, altered materially the régime of the Straits laid down in the Convention of 1923.[1] The chief beneficiaries of the revision were Turkey and Soviet Russia. Turkey, though still subject to an international servitude of free navigation through the Straits in peacetime, and in time of war when neutral, was freed from important limitations which the Lausanne Convention imposed on her when she was a belligerent. Turkish control over the Straits, although not absolute, was measurably strengthened by the disappearance of the demilitarization clauses of the 1923 Convention, the stricter regulation of the passage of non-military aircraft above the Straits and the abolition of the International Straits Commission whose duties and functions were transferred to the Turkish Government. What is even more important, Turkey when belligerent was relieved of all limitations and permitted to close the Straits to warships of all nations. True, Turkey's right to close the Straits to warships when threatened with "imminent danger of war" was subject to

[1] For the text of the Montreux Convention, see Appendix No. 3, p. 154.
Japan, no longer a member of the League of Nations, signed with a reservation in respect to exceptions provided for in Arts. 19 and 25 of the Convention in certain contingencies arising under the League Covenant.

a veto by a two-thirds vote of the League Council, but inasmuch as Turkey was then—and still is—a loyal member of the League with a semi-permanent seat on the Council, she was in fact not seriously handicapped by this limitation.

A no less important feature of the Montreux Convention was the satisfaction given to Russia's claims. The Black Sea Powers (and obviously in this category Russia alone needs to be taken into account for practical purposes) obtained the right to send warships through the Straits into the Aegean Sea without limitation of number, type or tonnage except that they must pass singly through the Straits. This provision conceded the time-honored Russian claim for unlimited egress from the Black Sea into the Mediterranean which Great Britain had always opposed unless full reciprocity were given to non-riparian powers. On the other hand, the limitations of the Lausanne treaty concerning the number and tonnage of naval forces which non-riparian Powers might send into the Black Sea in peacetime were revised as follows: the 1923 Convention limited the maximum force which *each* non-riparian Power might send into the Black Sea to the most powerful fleet of a riparian State—i.e., Russia. The Montreux Convention limits the *aggregate tonnage* of *all* non-riparian Powers to 30,000 tons [2] and the tonnage which any one non-riparian Power may send to two-thirds of the aggregate tonnage. Auxiliary vessels, carrying fuel and with specified arms only, are excepted from these limitations. The preponderant interests of the Black Sea Powers in general and of Russia in

[2] An "escalator" clause raised the limit to a maximum of 45,000 tons in the event that the tonnage of the strongest Black Sea fleet shall exceed by 10,000 tons the tonnage of the strongest fleet in that sea at the date of July 20, 1936—meaning of course the Russian fleet. Art. 18, par. 1 (b).

particular are further served by the provisions limiting the stay of non-riparian warships in the Black Sea to twenty-one days, and making "desirable" a notification of fifteen days for the transit of non-riparian warships, instead of the eight days required from riparian powers. In time of war, Turkey being neutral, neutral warships continue to enjoy free passage under the same conditions and limitations as govern passage in peace time; belligerent warships are not allowed transit except pursuant to rights or obligations of the signatories arising out of the League Covenant and in cases of assistance rendered to a State victim of aggression in virtue of a treaty of mutual assistance binding Turkey, provided that such treaty was concluded within the framework of the Covenant and registered and published in accordance with Art. 18 thereof. The signatories agreed that Turkey might begin refortification of the demilitarized zones on August 15. The Convention came in force upon the deposit of a sufficient number of ratifications on November 9, 1936.[3]

Thus, while the principle of freedom of navigation incorporated into both the Lausanne treaty and the Straits Convention of 1923 was reaffirmed at Montreux (indeed, Art. 28 of the Convention, limiting its duration to twenty years, specified that the principle should continue without time limit), it became subordinate to the security of Turkey and the Black Sea riparian states, primarily Soviet Russia. The extent to which this freedom might be enjoyed was

[3] For a detailed analysis of the Montreux Convention from the point of view of international law, see F. de Visscher, "La nouvelle Convention des Détroits," *Revue de droit international et de législation comparée*, Vol. 17 (3rd Ser.), pp. 669ff. (1936); Claude A. Colliard, "La Convention de Montreux, Nouvelle solution du problème des Détroits," *Revue de droit international*, Vol. 18, pp. 121ff. (1936).

greatly narrowed for non-riparian Powers; and the international control which under the 1923 Convention had the duty of insuring observance of rules gave way to control by the local sovereign. Whatever other merits the Montreux Convention may have had, it represented decidedly a step backward from the point of view of international administration, even though the door was left open to the . enforcement of the League Covenant—so long at least as Turkey remained a member of the League. For Russia it accomplished what successive attempts over the course of a century had failed to bring about: control of the Black Sea by the Russian fleet, freedom for Russia to send her raiders into the Mediterranean without danger of a superior force pursuing her into the Black Sea or in any way threatening her southern shores—with the exception of a punitive action undertaken against her under the League Covenant, a contingency which seemed very unlikely in the summer of 1936. So favorable a position for Russia was of course predicated upon the continuation of friendly relations with Turkey in the event of a war between Russia and other powers.

XIV.

FROM MONTREUX TO THE FRANCO–BRITISH–TURKISH MUTUAL ASSISTANCE PACT

THE arrangement achieved at Montreux was in general favorably received except in Italy and Germany. Great Britain made the most substantial sacrifice in the interest of a compromise by receding from her persistent policy of opposing a preferential status for Russia and the other Black Sea Powers. She apparently regarded the strengthening of Turko-British friendship and the consequent reinforcement of the balance in the Eastern Mediterranean, which had been disturbed by the establishment of Italian air and naval bases in the Dodecanese and an Italian empire in East Africa, as adequate compensation. France, allied with Russia, was not adverse to the increase of Soviet power; the Quai d'Orsay apparently proceeded on the assumption that Russia's improved position would bolster the chain of alliances which France had built up in Southeastern Europe and which had been materially weakened by the remilitarization of the Rhineland.

On the other hand, Italy and Germany were, for obvious reasons, displeased with the Montreux Convention. Italy, a party to the 1923 Convention, was resentful that the other signatories agreed to revision despite her absence—a fact which was felt to be derogatory to the influence claimed by Italy in world affairs. Moreover, the Fascist Government, genuinely apprehensive of communism, did not look with much favor upon the appearance of Soviet naval forces in the Mediterranean. Neither was Italy on too friendly terms with Turkey; for despite the treaty of friendship and repeated assurances of Mussolini, the Turks did not feel wholly secure as to the effect on their country of Italian imperial ambitions, a feeling of which Italy was well aware. Hence she could hardly have appreciated the increased power and prestige with which Turkey emerged from the Montreux Conference. An added reason for Italian displeasure was the belief (not without foundation) that concessions made by Great Britain and France to Turkey and Soviet Russia were motivated primarily by the desire of those powers to erect further barriers against Italian expansion.

Germany, at that time to all appearances the leading anti-communist power of Europe, professed to be primarily concerned about the advantageous position in which the Montreux Convention placed Soviet Russia. Collaterally, she was also disturbed by the possibility of increased Franco-British influence in Turkey and the resulting alignment of Turkey with the Western Allies which might hamper whatever ambitions she may have harbored in the Balkans and the Near East.

Nothing indicates more conclusively the growing strength of Turkey than the indifference shown by Angora toward the indications of displeasure by two major European powers. Even the absence of Italy's signature did not disturb the equanimity of the Turkish Government, although the full validity of the revised régime could technically be questioned so long as the signature of a party to the Lausanne Convention was lacking. The Turks doubtless realized that by regaining almost complete control over the Straits, they would henceforth be so important a factor in European diplomacy that not only could no Power afford to disregard them, but each would have to seek Turkey's good will and friendship. If the Turks made no particular efforts to secure Italy's approval on the assumption that they could afford to wait, their calculation proved to be correct. On May 2, 1938, Italy adhered to the Montreux Convention with reservations as to the discontinuance of her membership in the League of Nations, announced in December, 1937.[1]

The outbreak of the Spanish civil war a few days before the signature of the Montreux Convention diverted public attention from the significance of the new régime of the Straits. But the implications of Turkey's immensely strengthened position did not escape the chancellories of foreign offices. The diplomacy of European powers during the three years which have elapsed since the Montreux Convention came into force has not yet been revealed, and it is impossible to ascertain as yet from authentic sources what moves have taken place in this, as in many other respects. So long as there was any hope or expectation that a division of Europe into opposing ideological camps and a consequent return to the balance of power could be avoided—and this seems to have been the objective of Mr. Chamberlain's appeasement policy with respect to Italy's East African adventure, the Spanish civil war and the successive crises evoked by actions of the German Government—the pressing of Turkey's position into the foreground was clearly undesirable. But the moment such hopes disappeared—and, whether rightly or wrongly, the moment seems to have ar-

[1] See *Bulletin of International News*, 1938, p. 419.

rived when Germany substituted the "Lebensraum" theory for the principle of pure race in March, 1939—Turkey's attitude at once became of paramount importance. That the British and French Governments at least were not wholly inactive in the intervening period seems to be borne out by the rapidity with which an agreement in principle was reached with Turkey after the establishment of a German protectorate in Bohemia and Moravia. In the middle of May, 1939, the British Prime Minister announced to Parliament that consultations with Turkey had revealed the "customary identity of views" of the two Governments and the conclusion of a reciprocal mutual assistance treaty was contemplated.[2] A declaration of mutual assistance was signed by representatives of the French and Turkish Governments on June 23rd in wording almost identical with that announced by Mr. Chamberlain.[3] In both instances, the declaration specified that the contemplated agreement was not directed against any country but was aimed at assuring reciprocal assistance in the event of an act of aggression which might lead to war in the Mediterranean. The consultation also extended to assuring the establishment of security in the Balkans.

The significance of these declarations should be appreciated in the light of events which took place simultaneously. Abandoning the appeasement policy, Great Britain announced in the spring of 1939 her intention to extend, jointly with France, active assistance to Poland and, later, to Greece and Rumania in case of aggression. It was in order to render these assurances effective that consultations and negotiations were initiated between the Western Allies

[2] *Bulletin of International News*, 1939, p. 499.
[3] *Ibid.*, p. 658.

and Turkey and Soviet Russia respectively. The consultations with Turkey brought results quickly, even though the declarations merely recorded agreements in principle and the working out of details was left as a hurdle still to be surmounted. As is common knowledge, the negotiations with Soviet Russia came to naught. It would be idle to speculate whether the resounding diplomatic defeat of Great Britain and France in Moscow was due to inadequate preparation on their part, to the superior skill of Herr von Ribbentrop or to the duplicity of Soviet diplomacy. There are strong indications that the Soviet Government had entered into the negotiations with the Western Allies with its tongue in its cheek.

However that may be, the conclusion of the German-Soviet "non-aggression" pact and the complete and sudden shift in the alignment of European Powers was bound to bring Turkey into the limelight more than ever. Russia, which suddenly abandoned the collective security system and the pacific policy which she had professed so ardently in recent years to follow, found it of course necessary to assure, if possible, Turkish good will, if not cooperation, in the resumption of her imperial aspirations in the Baltic and the Balkans. Although no authentic information is available, it is reasonable to assume that during the four weeks of intermittent negotiations at the Kremlin, the Turkish Foreign Minister was presented with proposals intended to clinch for Russia the advantages secured by the Montreux Convention. Whether or not his reluctance to come to terms was motivated by the spectre of the dream of Peter the Great and Catherine II, however different an aspect that dream may now present, is as yet impossible to state. The importance which Germany attached to Turkey's position is shown by the choice of former Chancellor von Papen, who had played a leading rôle in preparing for the absorption of Austria and whose skill as a diplomat, in German eyes at least, was exceptional, as special ambassador to Turkey. The extent of pressure exerted by Great Britain and France in Angora is also unknown; but events have proved that neither the supplications of the Soviet statesmen nor the efforts of Herr von Papen on Germany's behalf were sufficiently attractive to move the Turks from the principle of mutual assistance agreed upon between Great Britain, France and Turkey in the spring of 1939.

A few days after the return of the Turkish Foreign Minister from Moscow, on October 19, 1939, a treaty of mutual assistance of fifteen years' duration, between Turkey, Great Britain and France, was signed at Angora [4] which brought Turkey definitely, although with important reservations, into the Allied camp. The Allies agreed to assist Turkey in case of aggression by a European power, while Turkey agreed to assist Great Britain and France (a) in case of an act of aggression by a European power leading to war in the Mediterranean and (b) in case those two countries should become engaged in hostilities on account of the guarantees given to Greece and Rumania in April, 1939. Turkey's commitments are substantially qualified by Protocol No. 2, signed simultaneously with the treaty, which releases her from taking action "having as its effect or involving as its consequence entry into armed conflict with the U.S.S.R." Arts. 4 and 5 provide for consultation in case of aggression not specifically involving active participation and secure for Great Britain and France "at least" Turkey's benevolent neutrality in case of aggression against either of

[4] For the text, see Appendix No. 4, p. 168.

these two states. The pact was put into force as of the date of its signature, without awaiting ratification (which, however, has been since accomplished) and was followed immediately by military consultations and the extension of large credits by the Western Allies to Turkey.

Judging from the reactions of the controlled German and Soviet press, the tripartite mutual assistance pact was not well received in Berlin and Moscow. The stipulation in the pact that it is not directed against any state and would be operative only in case of aggression, was given no credence by Germany and Soviet Russia. The saving clause in Protocol No. 2, exempting Turkey from action involving her in hostilities with Soviet Russia and the assertion of continued Turko-Soviet friendship by members of the Turkish Government, does not seem to have offset the Kremlin's disappointment over its failure to bring Turkey in line with the reincarnated imperial ambitions of the Soviet. Italy, technically linked with the axis powers, was cautious in expressing her reaction to the pact, although she probably should not rejoice over the advantage gained by the democratic powers. On the other hand, if Italy is more sincere in her professed anti-comintern policy than her partner in the Rome-Berlin axis proved to be, she probably regards as a gain the check on Russian ambitions in the Balkans which the pact doubtless imposed.

For the saving clause of Protocol No. 2 does not mean that Turkey will remain necessarily inactive, irrespective of Russia's conduct. True, she is not *compelled* to take action involving her in hostilities with Soviet Russia. In terms of practical politics, this means that even though war should break out between the Western Allies and the Soviet, Turkey is under no obligation to close the Straits against

Russia or to permit the Allies to send naval forces into the Black Sea in excess of the limitations laid down in the Montreux Convention. But there is nothing to prevent Turkey from adopting a different policy should she feel threatened by Russia or should the latter put forward demands on Turkey, in prosecution of the war with the Allies, which the Turks would consider incompatible with their security, their control over the Straits or with their national interest. In other words, it appears that the operation of the saving clause depends entirely on the conduct of Soviet Russia toward Turkey; more than ever, Russia ought to seek Turkey's friendship and good will, unless she feels strong enough to incur her hostility, with all the consequences that would involve.

The question of the control of the Straits by Turkey has not yet been squarely raised in the present war. Nevertheless, it is this control which makes the change of alignment by Turkey of such fundamental importance to Europe. Soviet Russia has evidently again embarked upon a policy of expansion. Her first positive steps have been in the direction of the northwest, culminating in the war with Finland. Whatever may be the outcome in the Baltic, there is ample evidence that Russia has by no means abandoned her ambitions in the south. The Allies have shown that despite their obvious reluctance to increase the number of their enemies, their support of Turkey in that eventuality does not exclude major military (and of course naval) cooperation. This would also be true if Germany, stalemated on the Western Front, should seek space for decisive action in Southeastern Europe. Once more, as in the past, the supreme strategic importance of the control of the Straits is abundantly evident. The impending crisis involves also Turkey's neighbors in the Balkans who would have to be overpowered or won over before either Germany or Russia could effectively challenge Turkish control. The pressure to which these Balkan nations are subjected from every side has apparently evoked among them, despite their traditional quarrels and distrust, a newly found sense of solidarity based on common economic and social interests in the preservation of their precarious peace which may lead to the formation of a new entente. It is highly significant that in this evolving situation Turkey is playing a leading part.

Unless the unexpected happens and the war ends shortly, one can be reasonably certain that the question of the Straits will be raised in one form or another. When and how this will occur it would be dangerous to prophesy; but despite the fact that so much of the unforeseen and unexpected has happened in our time, it is safe to predict that if and when the issue is raised, either during or after the war, we will see Great Britain, Russia and Turkey at the three corners of the triangle which so many times in history has constituted a graphic representation of the struggle to solve satisfactorily what has proved to be as impossible a task for European diplomacy as was the squaring of the circle for the mathematicians.

APPENDIX NO. 1

Treaty of Peace Between the Allied Powers and Turkey

Signed at Sèvres, August 10, 1920

Text from *British Treaty Series*, No. 11 (1920), Cmd. 964 [1]

Political Clauses

Section I.—*Constantinople*

Article 36

Subject to the provisions of the present Treaty, the High Contracting Parties agree that the rights and title of the Turkish Government over Constantinople shall not be affected, and that the said Government and His Majesty the Sultan shall be entitled to reside there and to maintain there the capital of the Turkish State.

Nevertheless, in the event of Turkey failing to observe faithfully the provisions of the present Treaty, or of any treaties or conventions supplementary thereto, particularly as regards the protection of the rights of racial, religious or linguistic minorities, the Allied Powers expressly reserve the right to modify the above provisions, and Turkey hereby agrees to accept any dispositions which may be taken in this connection.

[1] The text of the treaty can also be found in *The Treaties of Peace, 1919–1923* (publication of the Carnegie Endowment for International Peace, New York, 1924), Vol. 2, pp. 789ff.

Section II.—*Straits*

ARTICLE 37

The navigation of the Straits, including the Dardanelles, the Sea of Marmora and the Bosphorus, shall in future be open, both in peace and war, to every vessel of commerce or of war and to military and commercial aircraft, without distinction of flag.

These waters shall not be subject to blockade, nor shall any belligerent right be exercised nor any act of hostility be committed within them, unless in pursuance of a decision of the Council of the League of Nations.

ARTICLE 38

The Turkish Government recognises that it is necessary to take further measures to ensure the freedom of navigation provided for in Article 37, and accordingly delegates, so far as it is concerned, to a Commission to be called the "Commission of the Straits," and hereinafter referred to as "the Commission," the control of the waters specified in Article 39.

The Greek Government, so far as it is concerned, delegates to the Commission the same powers and undertakes to give it in all respects the same facilities.

Such control shall be exercised in the name of the Turkish and Greek Governments respectively, and in the manner provided in this Section.

ARTICLE 39

The authority of the Commission will extend to all the waters between the Mediterranean mouth of the Dardanelles and the Black Sea mouth of the Bosphorus, and to the waters within three miles of each of these mouths.

This authority may be exercised on shore to such extent as may be necessary for the execution of the provisions of this Section.

ARTICLE 40

The Commission shall be composed of representatives appointed respectively by the United States of America (if and when that Government is willing to participate), the British Empire, France, Italy, Japan, Russia (if and when Russia becomes a member of the League of Nations), Greece, Roumania, and Bulgaria and Turkey (if and when the two latter States become members of the League of Nations). Each Power shall appoint one representative. The representatives of the United States of America, the British Empire, France, Italy, Japan and Russia shall each have two votes. The representatives of Greece, Roumania, and Bulgaria and Turkey shall each have one vote. Each Commissioner shall be removable only by the Government which appointed him.

ARTICLE 42

The Commission will exercise the powers conferred on it by the present Treaty in complete independence of the local authority. It will have its own flag, its own budget and its separate organisation.

ARTICLE 44

In the event of the Commission finding that the liberty of passage is being interfered with, it will inform the representatives at Constantinople of the Allied Powers providing the occupying forces provided for in Article 178. These representatives will thereupon concert with the naval and military commanders of the said forces such measures as may be deemed necessary to preserve the freedom of the Straits. Similar action shall be taken by the said representatives in the event of any external action threatening the liberty of passage of the Straits.

ARTICLE 48

In order to facilitate the execution of the duties with which it is entrusted by this Section, the Commission shall have power to organise such a force of special police as may be necessary. This force shall be drawn so far as possible from the native population of the zone of the Straits and islands referred to in Article 178, Part V (Military, Naval and Air Clauses), excluding the islands of Lemnos, Imbros, Samothrace, Tenedos and Mitylene. The said force shall be commanded by foreign police officers appointed by the Commission.

ARTICLE 56

Ships of war in transit through the waters specified in Article 39 shall conform in all respects to the regulations issued by the Commission for the observance of the ordinary rules of navigation and of sanitary requirements.

ARTICLE 57

(1) Belligerent warships shall not revictual nor take in stores, except so far as may be strictly necessary to enable them to complete the passage of the Straits and to reach the nearest port where they can call, nor shall they replenish or increase their supplies of war material or their armament or complete their crews, within the waters under the control of the Commission. Only such repairs as are absolutely necessary to render them seaworthy shall be carried out, and they shall not add in any manner whatever to their fighting force. The Commission shall decide what repairs are necessary, and these must be carried out with the least possible delay.

(2) The passage of belligerent warships through the waters under the control of the Commission shall be effected with the least possible delay, and without any other interruption than that resulting from the necessities of the service.

(3) The stay of such warships at ports within the jurisdiction of the Commission shall not exceed twenty-four hours except in case of distress. In such case they shall be bound to leave as soon as possible. An interval of at least twenty-four hours shall always elapse between the sailing of a belligerent

ship from the waters under the control of the Commission and the departure of a ship belonging to an opposing belligerent.

(4) Any further regulations affecting in time of war the waters under the control of the Commission, and relating in particular to the passage of war material and contraband destined for the enemies of Turkey, or revictualling, taking in stores or carrying out repairs in the said waters, will be laid down by the League of Nations.

ARTICLE 58

Prizes shall in all respects be subjected to the same conditions as belligerent vessels of war.

ARTICLE 59

No belligerent shall embark or disembark troops, munitions of war or warlike materials in the waters under the control of the Commission, except in case of accidental hindrance of the passage, and in such cases the passage shall be resumed with all possible despatch.

ARTICLE 60

Nothing in Articles 57, 58 or 59 shall be deemed to limit the powers of a belligerent or belligerents acting in pursuance of a decision by the Council of the League of Nations.

APPENDIX NO. 2

CONVENTION ON THE RÉGIME OF THE STRAITS
Signed at Lausanne, July 24, 1923

Text from *League of Nations Treaty Series*, Vol. 28, p. 115 [1]

ART. 1. The High Contracting Parties agree to recognise and declare the principle of freedom of transit and of navigation by sea and by air in the Strait of the Dardanelles, the Sea of Marmora and the Bosphorus, hereinafter comprised under the general term of the "Straits."

ART. 2. The transit and navigation of commercial vessels and aircraft, and of war vessels and aircraft in the Straits in time of peace and in time of war shall henceforth be regulated by the provisions of the attached Annex.

ANNEX

RULES FOR THE PASSAGE OF COMMERCIAL VESSELS AND AIRCRAFT, AND OF WAR VESSELS AND AIRCRAFT THROUGH THE STRAITS

1. *Merchant Vessels, including Hospital Ships, Yachts and Fishing Vessels and non-Military Aircraft.*

(a) *In Time of Peace.*

Complete freedom of navigation and passage by day and by night under any flag and with any kind of cargo, without

---

[1] The text of the Convention can also be found in *British Treaty Series*, No. 16 (1923), Cmd. 1929, pp. 109ff.; *British and Foreign State Papers*, Vol. 117, p. 592; Hudson, *International Legislation*, Vol. 2, p. 1028.

any formalities, or tax, or charge whatever (subject, however, to international sanitary provisions) unless for services
directly rendered, such as pilotage, light, towage or other
similar charges, and without prejudice to the rights exercised
in this respect by the services and undertakings now operating
under concessions granted by the Turkish Government.

To facilitate the collection of these dues, merchant vessels
passing the Straits will communicate to stations appointed by
the Turkish Government their name, nationality, tonnage and
destination.

Pilotage remains optional.

(b) In Time of War, Turkey being Neutral.

Complete freedom of navigation and passage by day and by
night under the same conditions as above. The duties and
rights of Turkey as a neutral Power cannot authorise her to
take any measures liable to interfere with navigation through
the Straits, the waters of which, and the air above which, must
remain entirely free in time of war, Turkey being neutral just
as in time of peace.

Pilotage remains optional.

(c) In Time of War, Turkey being a Belligerent.

Freedom of navigation for neutral vessels and neutral non-
military aircraft, if the vessel or aircraft in question does not
assist the enemy, particularly by carrying contraband, troops
or enemy nationals. Turkey will have the right to visit and
search such vessels and aircraft, and for this purpose aircraft
are to alight on the ground or on the sea in such areas as are
specified and prepared for this purpose by Turkey. The rights
of Turkey to apply to enemy vessels the measures allowed by
international law are not affected.

Turkey will have full power to take such measures as she
may. consider necessary to prevent enemy vessels from using
the Straits. These measures, however, are not to be of such

a nature as to prevent the free passage of neutral vessels, and Turkey agrees to provide such vessels with either the necessary instructions or pilots for the above purpose.

2. *Warships, including Fleet Auxiliaries, Troopships, Aircraft Carriers and Military Aircraft.*

(a)   *In Time of Peace.*

Complete freedom of passage by day and by night under any flag, without any formalities, or tax, or charge whatever, but subject to the following restrictions as to the total force:

The maximum force which any one Power may send through the Straits into the Black Sea is not to be greater than that of the most powerful fleet of the littoral Powers of the Black Sea existing in that sea at the time of passage; but with the proviso that the Powers reserve to themselves the right to send into the Black Sea at all times and under all circumstances, a force of not more than three ships, of which no individual ship shall exceed 10,000 tons.

Turkey has no responsibility in regard to the number of war vessels which pass through the Straits.

In order to enable the above rule to be observed, the Straits Commission provided for in Article 10 will, on the 1st January and the 1st July of each year, enquire of each Black Sea littoral Power the number of each of the following classes of vessel which such Power possesses in the Black Sea: Battleships, battle-cruisers, aircraft-carriers, cruisers, destroyers, submarines, or other types of vessels as well as naval aircraft; distinguishing between the ships which are in active commission and the ships with reduced complements, the ships in reserve and the ships undergoing repairs or alterations.

The Straits Commission will then inform the Powers concerned that the strongest naval force in the Black Sea comprises: Battleships, battle-cruisers, aircraft-carriers, cruisers, destroyers, submarines, aircraft and units of other types which may exist. The Straits Commission will also immediately inform the Powers concerned when, owing to the passage into or out of the Black Sea of any ship of the strongest Black Sea force, any alteration in that force has taken place.

The naval force that may be sent through the Straits into the Black Sea will be calculated on the number and type of the ships of war in active commission only.

(b) In Time of War, Turkey being Neutral.

Complete freedom of passage by day and by night under any flag, without any formalities, or tax, or charge whatever, under the same limitations as in paragraph 2 (*a*).

However, these limitations will not be applicable to any belligerent Power to the prejudice of its belligerent rights in the Black Sea.

The rights and duties of Turkey as a neutral Power cannot authorise her to take any measures liable to interfere with navigation through the Straits, the waters of which, and the air above which, must remain entirely free in time of war, Turkey being neutral, just as in time of peace.

Warships and military aircraft of belligerents will be forbidden to make any capture, to exercise the right of visit and search, or to carry out any other hostile act in the Straits.

As regards revictualling and carrying out repairs, war vessels will be subject to the terms of the Thirteenth Hague Convention of 1907, dealing with maritime neutrality.

Military aircraft will receive in the Straits similar treatment to that accorded under the Thirteenth Hague Convention of 1907 to warships, pending the conclusion of an international Convention establishing the rules of neutrality for aircraft.

(c) In Time of War, Turkey being Belligerent.

Complete freedom of passage for neutral warships, without any formalities, or tax, or charge whatever, but under the same limitations as in paragraph 2 (*a*).

The measures taken by Turkey to prevent enemy ships and aircraft from using the Straits are not to be of such a nature as to prevent the free passage of neutral ships and aircraft, and Turkey agrees to provide the said ships and aircraft with either the necessary instructions or pilots for the above purpose.

Neutral military aircraft will make the passage of the Straits at their own risk and peril, and will submit to investigation as to their character. For this purpose aircraft are to alight on the ground or on the sea in such areas as are specified and prepared for this purpose by Turkey.

3. (*a*) The passage of the Straits by submarines of Powers at peace with Turkey must be made on the surface.

(*b*) The officer in command of a foreign naval force, whether coming from the Mediterranean or the Black Sea, will communicate, without being compelled to stop, to a signal station at the entrance to the Dardanelles or the Bosphorus, the number and the names of vessels under his orders which are entering the Straits.

These signal stations shall be notified from time to time by Turkey; until such signal stations are notified, the freedom of passage for foreign war vessels in the Straits shall not thereby be prejudiced, nor shall their entry into the Straits be for this reason delayed.

(*c*) The right of military and non-military aircraft to fly over the Straits, under the conditions laid down in the present rules, necessitates for aircraft—

(*i*) Freedom to fly over a strip of territory of five kilometres wide on each side of the narrow parts of the Straits;

(*ii*) Liberty, in the event of a forced landing, to alight on the coast or on the sea in the territorial waters of Turkey.

4. *Limitation of Time of Transit for Warships.*

In no event shall warships in transit through the Straits, except in the event of damage or peril of the sea, remain therein beyond the time which is necessary for them to effect their passage, including the time of anchorage during the night if necessary for safety of navigation.

5. *Stay in the Ports of the Straits and of the Black Sea.*

(*a*) Paragraphs 1, 2 and 3 of this Annex apply to the passage of vessels, warships and aircraft through and over the Straits and do not affect the right of Turkey to make such regulations as she may consider necessary regarding the number of men-of-war and military aircraft of any one Power which may visit Turkish ports or aerodromes at one time, and the duration of their stay.

(*b*) Littoral Powers of the Black Sea will also have a similar right as regards their ports and aerodromes.

(*c*) The light-vessels which the Powers at present represented on the European Commission of the Danube maintain as *stationnaires* at the mouths of that river as far up as Galatz will be regarded as additional to the men-of-war referred to in paragraph 2, and may be replaced in case of need.

6. *Special Provisions relating to Sanitary Protection.*

Warships which have on board cases of plague, cholera or typhus, or which have had such cases on board during the last seven days, and warships which have left an infected port within less than five times 24 hours must pass through the Straits in quarantine and apply by the means on board such prophylactic measures as are necessary to prevent any possibility of the Straits being infected.

The same rule shall apply to merchant ships having a doctor on board and passing straight through the Straits without calling at a port or breaking bulk.

Merchant ships not having a doctor on board shall be obliged to comply with the international sanitary regulations before entering the Straits, even if they are not to call at a port therein.

Warships and merchant vessels calling at one of the ports in the Straits shall be subject in that port to the international sanitary regulations applicable in the port in question.

ART. 3. With a view to maintaining the Straits free from any obstacle to free passage and navigation, the provisions contained in Articles 4 to 9 will be applied to the waters and shores thereof as well as to the islands situated therein, or in the vicinity.

ART. 4. The zones and islands indicated below shall be demilitarised:

1. Both shores of the Straits of the Dardanelles and the Bosphorus over the extent of the zones delimited below (see the attached map): [2]

Dardanelles:

On the north-west, the Gallipoli Peninsula and the area southeast of a line traced from a point on the Gulf of Xeros 4 kilometres northeast of Bakla-Burnu, reaching the Sea of Marmora at Kumbaghi and passing south of Kavak (this village excluded);

On the south-east, the area included between the coast and a line 20 kilometres from the coast, starting from Cape Eski-Stamboul opposite Tenedos and reaching the Sea of Marmora at a point on the coast immediately north of Karabigha.

Bosphorus (without prejudice to the special provisions relating to Constantinople contained in Article 8):

On the east, the area extending up to a line 15 kilometres from the eastern shore of the Bosphorus;

On the west, the area up to a line 15 kilometres from the western shore of the Bosphorus.

2. All the islands in the Sea of Marmora, with the exception of the island of Emir Ali Adasi.

3. In the Ægean Sea, the islands of Samothrace, Lemnos, Imbros, Tenedos and Rabbit Islands.

[2] Omitted in *League of Nations Treaty Series* 1, Vol. 28.–Ed.

ART. 5. A Commission composed of four representatives appointed respectively by the Governments of France, Great Britain, Italy and Turkey shall meet within 15 days of the coming into force of the present Convention to determine on the spot the boundaries of the zone laid down in Article 4 (1).

The Governments represented on that Commission will pay the salaries of their respective representatives.

Any general expenses incurred by the Commission shall be borne in equal shares by the Powers represented thereon.

ART. 6. Subject to the provisions of Article 8 concerning Constantinople, there shall exist, in the demilitarised zones and islands, no fortifications, no permanent artillery organisation, no submarine engines of war other than submarine vessels, no military aerial organisation, and no naval base.

No armed forces shall be stationed in the demilitarised zones and islands except the police and gendarmerie forces necessary for the maintenance of order; the armament of such forces will be composed only of revolvers, swords, rifles and four Lewis guns per hundred men, and will exclude any artillery.

In the territorial waters of the demilitarised zones and islands, there shall exist no submarine engines of war other than submarine vessels.

Notwithstanding the preceding paragraphs Turkey will retain the right to transport her armed forces through the demilitarised zones and islands of Turkish territory, as well as through their territorial waters, where the Turkish fleet will have the right to anchor.

Moreover, in so far as the Straits are concerned, the Turkish Government shall have the right to observe by means of aeroplanes or balloons both the surface and the bottom of the sea. Turkish aeroplanes will always be able to fly over the waters of the Straits and the demilitarised zones of Turkish territory, and will have full freedom to alight therein, either on land or on sea.

In the demilitarised zones and islands and in their territorial waters, Turkey and Greece shall similarly be entitled to effect such movements of personnel as are rendered necessary for the instruction outside these zones and islands of the men recruited therein.

Turkey and Greece shall have the right to organise in the said zones and islands in their respective territories any system of observation and communication, both telegraphic, telephonic and visual. Greece shall be entitled to send her fleet into the territorial waters of the demilitarised Greek islands, but may not use these waters as a base of operations against Turkey nor for any military or naval concentration for this purpose.

ART. 7. No submarine engines of war other than submarine vessels shall be installed in the waters of the Sea of Marmora.

The Turkish Government shall not install any permanent battery or torpedo tubes, capable of interfering with the passage of the Straits, in the coastal zone of the European shore of the Sea of Marmora or in the coastal zone on the Anatolian shore situated to the east of the demilitarised zone of the Bosphorus as far as Darije.

ART. 8. At Constantinople, including for this purpose Stamboul, Pera, Galata, Scutari, as well as Princes' Islands, and in the immediate neighbourhood of Constantinople, there may be maintained for the requirements of the capital, a garrison with a maximum strength of 12,000 men. An arsenal and naval base may also be maintained at Constantinople.

ART. 9. If, in case of war, Turkey, or Greece, in pursuance of their belligerent rights, should modify in any way the provisions of demilitarisation prescribed above, they will be bound to re-establish as soon as peace is concluded the régime laid down in the present Convention.

ART. 10. There shall be constituted at Constantinople an International Commission composed in accordance with Article 12 and called the "Straits Commission."

ART. 11. The Commission will exercise its functions over the waters of the Straits.

ART. 12. The Commission shall be composed of a representative of Turkey, who shall be President, and representatives of France, Great Britain, Italy, Japan, Bulgaria, Greece, Roumania, Russia, and the Serb-Croat-Slovene State, in so far as these Powers are signatories of the present Convention, each of these Powers being entitled to representation as from its ratification of the said Convention.

The United States of America, in the event of their acceding to the present Convention, will also be entitled to have one representative on the Commission.

Under the same conditions any independent littoral States of the Black Sea which are not mentioned in the first paragraph of the present Article will possess the same right.

ART. 13. The Governments represented on the Commission will pay the salaries of their representatives. Any incidental expenditure incurred by the Commission will be borne by the said Governments in the proportion laid down for the division of the expenses of the League of Nations.

ART. 14. It will be the duty of the Commission to see that the provisions relating to the passage of warships and military aircraft are carried out; these provisions are laid down in paragraphs 2, 3 and 4 of the Annex to Article 2.

ART. 15. The Straits Commission will carry out its functions under the auspices of the League of Nations, and will address to the League an annual report giving an account of its activities, and furnishing all information which may be useful in the interests of commerce and navigation; with this object in view the Commission will place itself in touch with the departments of the Turkish Government dealing with navigation through the Straits.

ART. 16. It will be the duty of the Commission to prescribe

such regulations as may be necessary for the accomplishment of its task.

ART. 17. The terms of the present Convention will not infringe the right of Turkey to move her fleet freely in Turkish waters.

ART. 18. The High Contracting Parties, desiring to secure that the demilitarisation of the Straits and of the contiguous zones shall not constitute an unjustifiable danger to the military security of Turkey, and that no act of war should imperil the freedom of the Straits or the safety of the demilitarised zones, agree as follows:

Should the freedom of navigation of the Straits or the security of the demilitarised zones be imperilled by a violation of the provisions relating to freedom of passage, or by a surprise attack or some act of war or threat of war, the High Contracting Parties, and in any case France, Great Britain, Italy and Japan, acting in conjunction, will meet such violation, attack, or other act of war or threat of war, by all the means that the Council of the League of Nations may decide for this purpose.

So soon as the circumstance which may have necessitated the action provided for in the preceding paragraph shall have ended, the régime of the Straits as laid down by the terms of the present Convention shall again be strictly applied.

The present provision, which forms an integral part of those relating to the demilitarisation and to the freedom of the Straits, does not prejudice the rights and obligations of the High Contracting Parties under the Covenant of the League of Nations.

ART. 19. The High Contracting Parties will use every possible endeavour to induce non-signatory Powers to accede to the present Convention.

This adherence will be notified through the diplomatic channel to the Government of the French Republic, and by that Government to all signatory or adhering States. The adherence will take effect as from the date of notification to the French Government.

ART. 20. The present Convention shall be ratified. The ratifications shall be deposited at Paris as soon as possible.

APPENDIX NO. 3

Convention Regarding the Régime of the Straits

Signed at Montreux, July 20, 1936

Text from *British Treaty Series* No. 30 (1937), Cmd. 5551 [1]

His Majesty the King of the Bulgarians, the President of the French Republic, His Majesty the King of Great Britain, Ireland and the British Dominions beyond the Seas, Emperor of India, His Majesty the King of the Hellenes, His Majesty the Emperor of Japan, His Majesty the King of Roumania, the President of the Turkish Republic, the Central Executive Committee of the Union of Soviet Socialist Republics, and His Majesty the King of Yugoslavia;

Desiring to regulate transit and navigation in the Straits of the Dardanelles, the Sea of Marmora and the Bosphorus comprised under the general term "Straits" in such manner as to safeguard, within the framework of Turkish security and of the security, in the Black Sea, of the riparian States, the principle enshrined in article 23 of the Treaty of Peace signed at Lausanne on the 24th July, 1923;

Have resolved to replace by the present Convention the Convention signed at Lausanne on the 24th July, 1923, . . .

Article 1

The High Contracting Parties recognise and affirm the principle of freedom of transit and navigation by sea in the Straits.

[1] Printed also in *League of Nations Treaty Series,* Vol. 173, p. 213.

The Annexes to the Convention, being of a technical character, have not been reprinted.

The exercise of this freedom shall henceforth be regulated by the provisions of the present Convention.

Section I.—*Merchant Vessels*

ARTICLE 2

In time of peace, merchant vessels shall enjoy complete freedom of transit and navigation in the Straits, by day and by night, under any flag and with any kind of cargo, without any formalities, except as provided in article 3 below. No taxes or charges other than those authorised by Annex I to the present Convention shall be levied by the Turkish authorities on these vessels when passing in transit without calling at a port in the Straits.

In order to facilitate the collection of these taxes or charges merchant vessels passing through the Straits shall communicate to the officials at the stations referred to in article 3 their name, nationality, tonnage, destination and last port of call (provenance).

Pilotage and towage remain optional.

ARTICLE 3

All ships entering the Straits by the Ægean Sea or by the Black Sea shall stop at a sanitary station near the entrance to the Straits for the purposes of the sanitary control prescribed by Turkish law within the framework of international sanitary regulations. This control, in the case of ships possessing a clean bill of health or presenting a declaration of health testifying that they do not fall within the scope of the provisions of the second paragraph of the present article, shall be carried out by day and by night with all possible speed, and the vessels in question shall not be required to make any other stop during their passage through the Straits.

Vessels which have on board cases of plague, cholera, yellow fever, exanthematic typhus or smallpox, or which have had such cases on board during the previous seven days, and vessels which have left an infected port within less than five times twenty-four hours shall stop at the sanitary stations indicated in the preceding paragraph in order to embark such sanitary guards as the Turkish authorities may direct. No tax or charge shall be levied in respect of these sanitary guards and they shall be disembarked at a sanitary station on departure from the Straits.

ARTICLE 4

In time of war, Turkey not being belligerent, merchant vessels, under any flag or with any kind of cargo, shall enjoy freedom of transit and navigation in the Straits subject to the provisions of articles 2 and 3.

Pilotage and towage remain optional.

ARTICLE 5

In time of war, Turkey being belligerent, merchant vessels not belonging to a country at war with Turkey shall enjoy freedom of transit and navigation in the Straits on condition that they do not in any way assist the enemy.

Such vessels shall enter the Straits by day and their transit shall be effected by the route which shall in each case be indicated by the Turkish authorities.

ARTICLE 6

Should Turkey consider herself to be threatened with imminent danger of war, the provisions of article 2 shall nevertheless continue to be applied except that vessels must enter the Straits by day and that their transit must be effected by the route which shall, in each case, be indicated by the Turkish authorities.

Pilotage may, in this case, be made obligatory, but no charge shall be levied.

ARTICLE 7

The term "merchant vessels" applies to all vessels which are not covered by Section II of the present Convention.

Section II.—*Vessels of War*

ARTICLE 8

For the purposes of the present Convention, the definitions of vessels of war and of their specification together with those relating to the calculation of tonnage shall be as set forth in Annex II to the present Convention.

ARTICLE 9

Naval auxiliary vessels specifically designed for the carriage of fuel, liquid or non-liquid, shall not be subject to the provisions of article 13 regarding notification, nor shall they be counted for the purpose of calculating the tonnage which is subject to limitation under articles 14 and 18, on condition that they shall pass through the Straits singly. They shall, however, continue to be on the same footing as vessels of war for the purpose of the remaining provisions governing transit.

The auxiliary vessels specified in the preceding paragraph shall only be entitled to benefit by the exceptional status therein contemplated if their armament does not include: for use against floating targets, more than two guns of a maximum calibre of 105 millimetres; for use against aerial targets, more than two guns of a maximum calibre of 75 millimetres.

ARTICLE 10

In time of peace, light surface vessels, minor war vessels and auxiliary vessels, whether belonging to Black Sea or non-Black Sea Powers, and whatever their flag, shall enjoy freedom of transit through the Straits without any taxes or charges whatever, provided that such transit is begun during daylight and subject to the conditions laid down in article 13 and the articles following thereafter.

Vessels of war other than those which fall within the categories specified in the preceding paragraph shall only enjoy a right of transit under the special conditions provided by articles 11 and 12.

ARTICLE 11

Black Sea Powers may send through the Straits capital ships of a tonnage greater than that laid down in the first paragraph of article 14, on condition that these vessels pass through the Straits singly, escorted by not more than two destroyers.

ARTICLE 12

Black Sea Powers shall have the right to send through the Straits, for the purpose of rejoining their base, submarines constructed or purchased outside the Black Sea, provided that adequate notice of the laying down or purchase of such submarines shall have been given to Turkey.

Submarines belonging to the said Powers shall also be entitled to pass through the Straits to be repaired in dockyards outside the Black Sea on condition that detailed information on the matter is given to Turkey.

In either case, the said submarines must travel by day and on the surface, and must pass through the Straits singly.

ARTICLE 13

The transit of vessels of war through the Straits shall be preceded by a notification given to the Turkish Government through the diplomatic channel. The normal period of notice shall be eight days; but is desirable that in the case of non-Black Sea Powers this period should be increased to fifteen days. The notification shall specify the destination, name, type and number of the vessels, as also the date of entry for the outward passage and, if necessary, for the return journey. Any change of date shall be subject to three days' notice.

Entry into the Straits for the outward passage shall take place within a period of five days from the date given in the original notification. After the expiry of this period, a new notification shall be given under the same conditions as for the original notification.

When effecting transit, the commander of the naval force shall, without being under any obligation to stop, communicate to a signal station at the entrance to the Dardanelles or the Bosphorus the exact composition of the force under his orders.

ARTICLE 14

The maximum aggregate tonnage of all foreign naval forces which may be in course of transit through the Straits shall not exceed 15,000 tons, except in the cases provided for in article 11 and in Annex III to the present Convention.

The forces specified in the preceding paragraph shall not, however, comprise more than nine vessels.

Vessels, whether belonging to Black Sea or non-Black Sea Powers, paying visits to a port in the Straits, in accordance with the provisions of article 17, shall not be included in this tonnage.

Neither shall vessels of war which have suffered damage during their passage through the Straits be included in this tonnage; such vessels, while undergoing repair, shall be subject to any special provisions relating to security laid down by Turkey.

ARTICLE 15

Vessels of war in transit through the Straits shall in no circumstances make use of any aircraft which they may be carrying.

ARTICLE 16

Vessels of war in transit through the Straits shall not, except in the event of damage or peril of the sea, remain therein longer than is necessary for them to effect the passage.

ARTICLE 17

Nothing in the provisions of the preceding articles shall prevent a naval force of any tonnage or composition from paying a courtesy visit of limited duration to a port in the Straits, at the invitation of the Turkish Government. Any such force must leave the Straits by the same route as that by which it entered, unless it fulfils the conditions required for passage in transit through the Straits as laid down by articles 10, 14 and 18.

ARTICLE 18

(1) The aggregate tonnage which non-Black Sea Powers may have in that sea in time of peace shall be limited as follows:—

(a) Except as provided in paragraph (b) below, the aggregate tonnage of the said Powers shall not exceed 30,000 tons;

(b) If at any time the tonnage of the strongest fleet in the Black Sea shall exceed by at least 10,000 tons the tonnage of the strongest fleet in that sea at the date of the signature of the present Convention, the aggregate tonnage of 30,000 tons mentioned in paragraph (a) shall be increased by the same amount, up to a maximum of 45,000 tons. For this purpose, each Black Sea Power shall, in conformity with Annex IV to the present Convention, inform the Turkish Government, on the 1st January and the 1st July of each year, of the total tonnage of its fleet in the Black Sea; and the Turkish Government shall transmit this information to the other High Contracting Parties and to the Secretary-General of the League of Nations.

(c) The tonnage which any one non-Black Sea Power may have in the Black Sea shall be limited to two-thirds of the aggregate tonnage provided for in paragraphs (a) and (b) above;

(d) In the event, however, of one or more non-Black Sea Powers desiring to send naval forces into the Black Sea, for a humanitarian purpose, the said forces, which shall in no case exceed 8,000 tons altogether, shall be allowed to enter the Black Sea without having to give the notification provided for in article 13 of the present Convention, provided an authorisation is obtained from the Turkish Government in the following circumstances: if the figure of the aggregate tonnage specified in paragraphs (a) and (b) above has not been reached and will not be exceeded by the despatch of the forces which it is desired to send, the Turkish Government shall grant the said authorisation within the shortest possible time after receiving the request which has been addressed to it; if the said figure has already been reached or if the despatch of the forces which it is desired to send will cause it to be exceeded, the Turkish Government will immediately inform the other Black Sea Powers of the request for authorisation, and if the said Powers make no objection within twenty-four hours of having received this information, the Turkish Government shall, within forty-eight hours at the latest, inform the interested Powers of the reply which it has decided to make to their request.

Any further entry into the Black Sea of naval forces of non-Black Sea Powers shall only be effected within the available limits of the aggregate tonnage provided for in paragraphs (a) and (b) above.

(2) Vessels of war belonging to non-Black Sea Powers shall not remain in the Black Sea more than twenty-one days, whatever be the object of their presence there.

ARTICLE 19

In time of war, Turkey not being belligerent, warships shall enjoy complete freedom of transit and navigation through the Straits under the same conditions as those laid down in articles 10 to 18.

Vessels of war belonging to belligerent Powers shall not, however, pass through the Straits except in cases arising out of the application of article 25 of the present Convention, and in cases of assistance rendered to a State victim of aggression in virtue of a treaty of mutual assistance binding Turkey, concluded within the framework of the Covenant of the League of Nations, and registered and published in accordance with the provisions of article 18 of the Covenant.

In the exceptional cases provided for in the preceding paragraph, the limitations laid down in articles 10 to 18 of the present Convention shall not be applicable.

Notwithstanding the prohibition of passage laid down in paragraph 2 above, vessels of war belonging to belligerent Powers, whether they are Black Sea Powers or not, which have become separated from their bases, may return thereto.

Vessels of war belonging to belligerent Powers shall not make any capture, exercise the right of visit and search, or carry out any hostile act in the Straits.

ARTICLE 20

In time of war, Turkey being belligerent, the provisions of articles 10 to 18 shall not be applicable; the passage of warships shall be left entirely to the discretion of the Turkish Government.

ARTICLE 21

Should Turkey consider herself to be threatened with imminent danger of war she shall have the right to apply the provisions of article 20 of the present Convention.

Vessels which have passed through the Straits before Turkey has made use of the powers conferred upon her by the preceding paragraph, and which thus find themselves separated from their bases, may return thereto. It is, however, understood that Turkey may deny this right to vessels of war belonging to the State whose attitude has given rise to the application of the present article.

Should the Turkish Government make use of the powers conferred by the first paragraph of the present article, a notification to that effect shall be addressed to the High Contracting Parties and to the Secretary-General of the League of Nations.

If the Council of the League of Nations decide by a majority of two-thirds that the measures thus taken by Turkey are not justified, and if such should also be the opinion of the majority of the High Contracting Parties signatories to the present Convention, the Turkish Government undertakes to discontinue the measures in question as also any measures which may have been taken under article 6 of the present Convention.

ARTICLE 22

Vessels of war which have on board cases of plague, cholera, yellow fever, exanthematic typhus or smallpox or which have had such cases on board within the last seven days and vessels of war which have left an infected port within less than five times twenty-four hours must pass through the Straits in quarantine and apply by the means on board such prophylactic measures as are necessary in order to prevent any possibility of the Straits being infected.

SECTION III.—*Aircraft*

ARTICLE 23

In order to assure the passage of civil aircraft between the Mediterranean and the Black Sea, the Turkish Government will indicate the air routes available for this purpose, outside the forbidden zones which may be established in the Straits. Civil aircraft may use these routes provided that they give the Turkish Government, as regards occasional flights, a notification of three days, and as regards flights on regular services, a general notification of the dates of passage.

The Turkish Government moreover undertake, notwithstanding any remilitarisation of the Straits, to furnish the necessary facilities for the safe passage of civil aircraft authorised under the air regulations in force in Turkey to fly across Turkish territory between Europe and Asia. The route which is to be followed in the Straits zone by aircraft which have obtained an authorisation shall be indicated from time to time.

Section IV.—*General Provisions*
ARTICLE 24

The functions of the International Commission set up under the Convention relating to the régime of the Straits of the 24th July, 1923, are hereby transferred to the Turkish Government.

The Turkish Government undertake to collect statistics and to furnish information concerning the application of articles 11, 12, 14 and 18 of the present Convention.

They will supervise the execution of all the provisions of the present Convention relating to the passage of vessels of war through the Straits.

As soon as they have been notified of the intended passage through the Straits of a foreign naval force the Turkish Government shall inform the representatives at Angora of the High Contracting Parties of the composition of that force, its tonnage, the date fixed for its entry into the Straits, and, if necessary, the probable date of its return.

The Turkish Government shall address to the Secretary-

General of the League of Nations and to the High Contracting Parties an annual report giving details regarding the movements of foreign vessels of war through the Straits and furnishing all information which may be of service to commerce and navigation, both by sea and by air, for which provision is made in the present Convention.

ARTICLE 25

Nothing in the present Convention shall prejudice the rights and obligations of Turkey, or of any of the other High Contracting Parties members of the League of Nations, arising out of the Covenant of the League of Nations.

Section V.—*Final Provisions*
ARTICLE 26

The present Convention shall be ratified as soon as possible.

The ratifications shall be deposited in the archives of the Government of the French Republic in Paris.

The Japanese Government shall be entitled to inform the Government of the French Republic through their diplomatic representative in Paris that the ratification has been given, and in that case they shall transmit the instrument of ratification as soon as possible.

A *procès-verbal* of the deposit of ratifications shall be drawn up as soon as six instruments of ratification, including that of Turkey, shall have been deposited. For this purpose the notification provided for in the preceding paragraph shall be taken as the equivalent of the deposit of an instrument of ratification.

The present Convention shall come into force on the date of the said *procès-verbal*.

The French Government will transmit to all the High Contracting Parties an authentic copy of the *procès-verbal* provided for in the preceding paragraph and of the *procès-verbaux* of the deposit of any subsequent ratifications.

ARTICLE 27

The present Convention shall, as from the date of its entry into force, be open to accession by any Power signatory to the Treaty of Peace at Lausanne signed on the 24th July, 1923.

Each accession shall be notified, through the diplomatic channel, to the Government of the French Republic, and by the latter to all the High Contracting Parties.

Accessions shall come into force as from the date of notification to the French Government.

ARTICLE 28

The present Convention shall remain in force for twenty years from the date of its entry into force.

The principle of freedom of transit and navigation affirmed in article 1 of the present Convention shall however continue without limit of time.

If, two years prior to the expiry of the said period of twenty years, no High Contracting Party shall have given notice of denunciation to the French Government the present Convention shall continue in force until two years after such notice shall have been given. Any such notice shall be communicated by the French Government to the High Contracting Parties.

In the event of the present Convention being denounced in accordance with the provisions of the present article, the High Contracting Parties agree to be represented at a conference for the purpose of concluding a new Convention.

ARTICLE 29

At the expiry of each period of five years from the date of the entry into force of the present Convention each of the High Contracting Parties shall be entitled to initiate a proposal for amending one or more of the provisions of the present Convention.

To be valid, any request for revision formulated by one of

the High Contracting Parties must be supported, in the case of modifications to articles 14 or 18, by one other High Contracting Party, and, in the case of modifications to any other article, by two other High Contracting Parties.

Any request for revision thus supported must be notified to all the High Contracting Parties three months prior to the expiry of the current period of five years. This notification shall contain details of the proposed amendments and the reasons which have given rise to them.

Should it be found impossible to reach an agreement on these proposals through the diplomatic channel, the High Contracting Parties agree to be represented at a conference to be summoned for this purpose.

Such a conference may only take decisions by a unanimous vote, except as regards cases of revision involving articles 14 and 18, for which a majority of three-quarters of the High Contracting Parties shall be sufficient.

The said majority shall include three-quarters of the High Contracting Parties which are Black Sea Powers, including Turkey.

APPENDIX NO. 4

TREATY OF MUTUAL ASSISTANCE BETWEEN HIS MAJESTY
IN RESPECT OF THE UNITED KINGDOM, THE PRESIDENT
OF THE FRENCH REPUBLIC AND THE PRESIDENT
OF THE TURKISH REPUBLIC

Signed at Angora, October 10, 1939

Text from *Department of State Bulletin*, Vol. I, No. 20, p. 544

(Translation)

The President of the French Republic, His Majesty The King of Great Britain, Ireland and the British Dominions beyond the Seas, Emperor of India (in respect of the United Kingdom of Great Britain and Northern Ireland), and the President of the Turkish Republic:

Desiring to conclude a treaty of a reciprocal character in the interests of their national security, and to provide for mutual assistance in resistance to aggression,

Have appointed as their Plenipotentiaries, namely:

The President of the French Republic:

> M. René Massigli, Ambassador Extraordinary and Plenipotentiary, Commander of the Legion of Honour;

His Majesty the King of Great Britain, Ireland and the British Dominions beyond the Seas, Emperor of India (in respect of the United Kingdom of Great Britain and Northern Ireland):

> Sir Hughe Montgomery Knatchbull-Hugessen, K.C.M.G., Ambassador Extraordinary and Plenipotentiary;

The President of the Turkish Republic:

> Dr. Refik Saydam, President of the Council, Minister for Foreign Affairs *ad int.*, Deputy for Istanbul.

Who, having communicated their full powers, found in good and due form, have agreed as follows:—

ARTICLE 1

In the event of Turkey being involved in hostilities with a European Power in consequence of aggression by that Power against Turkey, France and the United Kingdom will co-operate effectively with Turkey and will lend her all aid and assistance in their power.

ARTICLE 2

(1) In the event of an act of aggression by a European Power leading to war in the Mediterranean area in which France and the United Kingdom are involved, Turkey will collaborate effectively with France and the United Kingdom and will lend them all aid and assistance in its power.

(2) In the event of an act of aggression by a European Power leading to war in the Mediterranean area in which Turkey is involved, the Government of the United Kingdom and the French Government will collaborate effectively with the Turkish Government and will lend it all aid and assistance in their power.

ARTICLE 3

So long as the guarantees given by France and the United Kingdom to Greece and Roumania by their respective Declarations of the 13th April, 1939, remain in force, Turkey will co-operate effectively with France and the United Kingdom and will lend them all aid and assistance in its power, in the event of France and the United Kingdom being engaged in hostilities in virtue of either of the said guarantees.

ARTICLE 4

In the event of France and the United Kingdom being involved in hostilities with a European Power in consequence of aggression committed by that Power against either of those States without the provisions of Articles 2 or 3 being applicable, the High Contracting Parties will immediately consult together.

It is nevertheless agreed that in such an eventuality Turkey will observe at least a benevolent neutrality towards France and the United Kingdom.

ARTICLE 5

Without prejudice to the provisions of Article 3 above, in the event of either:

(1) aggression by a European Power against another European State which the Government of one of the High Contracting Parties had, with the approval of that State, undertaken to assist in maintaining its independence or neutrality against such aggression, or

(2) aggression by a European Power which, while directed against another European State, constituted, in the opinion of the Government of one of the High Contracting Parties, a menace to its own security,

the High Contracting Parties will immediately consult together with a view to such common action as might be considered effective.

ARTICLE 6

The present Treaty is not directed against any country, but is designed to assure France, the United Kingdom and Turkey of mutual aid and assistance in resistance to aggression should the necessity arise.

ARTICLE 7

The provisions of the present Treaty are equally binding as bilateral obligations between Turkey and each of the two other High Contracting Parties.

ARTICLE 8

If the High Contracting Parties are engaged in hostilities in consequence of the operation of the present Treaty, they will not conclude an armistice peace except by common agreement.

ARTICLE 9

The present Treaty shall be ratified and the instruments of ratification shall be deposited simultaneously at Angora as soon as possible. It shall enter into force on the date of this deposit.

The present Treaty is concluded for a period of fifteen years. If none of the High Contracting Parties has notified the two others of its intention to terminate it six months before the expiration of the said period, the Treaty will be renewed by tacit consent for a further period of five years, and so on.

PROTOCOL No. 1

The undersigned Plenipotentiaries state that their respective Governments agree that the Treaty of mutual assistance dated this day shall be put into force from the moment of its signature.

PROTOCOL No. 2

At the moment of signature of the Treaty between the United Kingdom, France and Turkey, the undersigned Plenipotentiaries, duly authorized to this effect, have agreed as follows:—

The obligations undertaken by Turkey in virtue of the above-mentioned Treaty cannot compel that country to take action having its effect, or involving as its consequence, entry into armed conflict with the U.S.S.R.

The present Protocol of Signature shall be considered as an integral part of the Treaty of Mutual Assistance concluded to-day between the United Kingdom, France and Turkey.

BIBLIOGRAPHY

(*Note:* This is not an exhaustive list of all documents and writings on the Straits question, but it is intended to be a select bibliography of the more important and useful source materials.)

GOVERNMENT PUBLICATIONS AND OTHER DOCUMENTARY
   SOURCES

Actes de la Conférence de Montreux. (Paris, 1936.)

British Documents on the Origins of the War, 1898–1914.
   11 vols. (London, 1924–26.)

British and Foreign State Papers. (Serial: published yearly
   since 1813.)

British Treaty Series.

Conférence de Lausanne. Documents diplomatiques. 2 vols.
   (Paris, 1923.) (Published by the French Ministry for
   Foreign Affairs.)

*Constantinople et les Détroits. Documents secrets de l'ancien
   Ministère des Affaires Etrangères de Russie.* 2 vols. (Paris,
   1930–32.) (Published by *La Documentation Interna-
   tionale.*) [This is a translation of the original Russian
   documents edited by E. A. Adamov and published in
   2 vols., Moscow, 1925–1926.]

Der diplomatische Schriftwechsel Izvolskis, 1911–1914, 4 vols.
   (Berlin, 1924.) [Edited for the German Foreign Office
   from the secret Russian State archives by F. Stieve.]

Die internationalen Beziehungen im Zeitalter des Imperialismus.
8 vols. in 11 parts. (Berlin, 1931–1936.) [Russian Documents relating to the World War in German translation;
edited by Otto Hoetzsch.]

Documents diplomatiques français. (Serial: published by the
French Ministry for Foreign Affairs.)

Affaires d'Orient. Congrès de Berlin, 1878. (Paris, 1878.)

Documents diplomatiques français, 1871–1914. 26 vols.
(Paris, 1929–1936.)

Documents on International Affairs. (Published yearly since
1928 by the Royal Institute of International Affairs,
London.)

Giannini, Amedeo, *I Documenti diplomatici della pace
orientale.* (Roma, 1922.)

Grosse Politik der europäischen Kabinette, 1871–1914, Die.
40 vols. (Berlin, 1922–1927.)

Hansard, Parliamentary Debates. (Great Britain.)

Lausanne Conference on Near Eastern Affairs. Cmd. 1814
(1923).

League of Nations Official Journal.

League of Nations Treaty Series.

Livre rouge. La question de Mossoul. (Turkish Red Book.)
(Constantinople, 1925.)

Martens, F. de, *Recueil des traités.*

—— *Nouveau recueil général des traités.*

Noradounghian, Gabriel, *Recueil d'actes internationaux de
l'Empire Ottoman.* 4 vols. (Paris, 1897–1903.)

*Österreich-Ungarns Aussenpolitik von der Bosnischen Krise
1908 bis zum Kriegsausbruch 1914. Diplomatische Ak-
tenstücke des österreichisch-ungarischen Ministerium des
Äussern.* 9 vols. (Wien, 1930.)

Pribram, A. F., The Secret Treaties of Austria-Hungary,
1879–1914. 2 vols. (Cambridge, Mass., 1920.)

Recueil de documents diplomatiques. Negotiations ayant précédé la guerre avec la Turquie. (Russia. Ministry for Foreign Affairs, Petrograd, 1915.)

Sessional Papers. (Great Britain.)

Un livre noir. Diplomatie d'avant-guerre d'après les documents des archives russes. (Edited by René Marchand.) 3 vols. (Paris, 1922–34.)

United States Foreign Relations. (Serial: published yearly since 1861 by the Department of State, Washington, D. C.)

BIOGRAPHIES, MONOGRAPHS AND TREATISES

Bogićević, M., *Kriegsursachen.* (Zürich, 1919.)

Buchanan, Sir George, My Mission to Russia and Other Diplomatic Memoirs. 2 vols. (London, 1923.)

Dascovici, Nicolas, *La question du Bosphore et des Dardanelles.* (Geneva, 1915.)

Fay, Sidney B., The Origins of the World War. 2d rev. ed. (New York, 1930.)

Fuad, Ali, *La question des Détroits.* (Paris, 1928.)

Geshov, I. E., The Balkan League. (London, 1915.)

Gooch, George P., History of Modern Europe, 1878–1919. (London, 1923.)

Goriainov, Sergeii, *Le Bosphore et les Dardanelles.* (Paris, 1910.)

Grey, Viscount of Fallodon, Twenty-Five Years, 1892–1916. 2 vols. (New York, 1925.)

Holland, T. E., The Treaty Relations of Russia and Turkey. (London, 1877.)

Howard, Harry N., The Partition of Turkey. A Diplomatic History, 1913–1923. (Norman, Okla., 1931.)

Lansing, Robert, The Peace Negotiations. (Boston, 1921.)

Mandelstam, André N., *La politique Russe d'accès à la Méditer-*

ranée au XXème siècle. Académie de droit international à La Haye, *Recueil des cours*, Vol. 47 (1934. I), pp. 603–798.)

Marriott, Sir John A. R., The Eastern Question. (Oxford, 1924.)

Mischef, P., *La Mer Noire et les détroits de Constantinople.* (Paris, 1899.)

Noel-Buxton, Edward, Balkan Problems and European Peace. (London, 1919.)

Out of My Past. The Memoirs of Count Kokovtsov. Edited by H. H. Fisher. (Stanford Univ., Cal., 1935.) [Hoover War Library Publications No. 6.]

Paléologue, M., An Ambassador's Memoirs. 3 vols. (London, 1923.)

Phillipson, C., and Buxton, N., The Question of the Bosphorus and the Dardanelles. (London, 1917.)

Poincaré, Raymond, *Au service de la France.* 10 vols. (Paris, 1926–1933.)

Sazonow, S. D., Fateful Years. (New York, 1928.)

Schlesinger, Nathan, *Nouveau régime des Détroits.* (Paris, 1926.)

Schmitt, Bernadotte E., The Coming of the War, 1914. 2 vols. (New York, 1930.)

Stieve, F., Isvolski and the World War. Transl. by Dickes. (New York, 1926.)

Survey of International Affairs. (Serial: published yearly since 1924 by the Royal Institute for International Affairs.)

Taube, Baron M. de, *La politique russe d'avant-guerre et la fin de l'empire des Tsars (1904–1917).* (Paris, 1928.)

Temperley, H. W. V., A History of the Peace Conference of Paris. Vol. VI. (London, 1924.)

Three Peace Congresses of the Nineteenth Century. (Cambridge, Mass., 1917.)

Wirthwein, Walter G., Britain and the Balkan Crisis, 1875–1878. (New York, 1935.) (Studies in History, Economics and Public Law, Faculty of Political Science of Columbia University, No. 407.)

Woodward, E. L., The Congress of Berlin, 1878. (London, 1920.) (Handbook prepared under the Direction of the Historical Section of the Foreign Office, No. 154.)

PERIODICAL LITERATURE

Colliard, Claude A., "*La Convention de Montreux, Nouvelle solution du probleme des Détroits*," *Revue de droit international*, Vol. 18, pp. 121ff. (1936).

Cummings, A. N., "The Secret History of the Treaty of Berlin," *Nineteenth Century*, Vol. 58, pp. 83ff. (1905).

Driault, E., "*La question d'Orient en 1807*," *Revue d'histoire diplomatique*, Vol. 14, pp. 436ff. (1900).

Florinsky, M. T., "Russia and Constantinople: Count Kokovtzov's Evidence," *Foreign Affairs*, Vol. 8, pp. 135ff. (1930).

——, "A Page of Diplomatic History: Russian Military Leaders and the Problem of Constantinople during the War," *Political Science Quarterly*, Vol. 44, pp. 108ff. (1929).

Kerner, R. J., "Russia, the Straits and Constantinople," *Journal of Modern History*, Vol. 1, pp. 400ff. (1929).

"The Mission of Liman von Sanders," *Slavonic Review*, Vol. 6, pp. 12ff., 344ff., 543ff.; Vol. 7, pp. 90ff. (1927–28).

Langer, W. L., "Russia, the Straits Question and the Origins of the Balkan League," *Political Science Quarterly*, Vol. 43, pp. 321ff. (1928).

Rougier, Antoine, "*La question des Détroits et la Convention de Lausanne*," *Revue général de droit international public*, Vol. 31, pp. 309ff. (1924).

Visscher, Fernand de, "*Nouveau régime des Détroits,*" *Revue de droit international et de législation comparée,* Vol. 4 (3rd Ser.), pp. 537ff. (1923); Vol. 5, pp. 13ff. (1924).

"*La nouvelle Convention des Détroits,*" *Revue de droit international et de législation comparée,* Vol. 17 (3rd Ser.), pp. 669ff. (1936).

CHRONOLOGICAL INDEX OF TREATIES, CONVENTIONS AND AGREEMENTS

GENERAL INDEX

Abbasid caliphs, 10

Abydos, 2, 3

Adrianople: capital of Ottoman Turks *1367*, 8; fall of, *1878*, 58; Russian opposition to annexation by Bulgaria, 90

Aegean Sea: center of Greek interest, 1–3; Turkish naval forces, 45; strategic islands, 91, 116; unlimited egress from Black Sea conceded to Russia, 125

Aegospotami, 3

Aerenthal, Count Alois, Austro-Hungarian Foreign Minister (1906–12): announcement of Sandjak railway line, 77; Buchlau conversations, 79, 80; annexation of Bosnia and Herzegovina, 81, 82, 85

Afghanistan, 73

Africa, North: corsair power, 10; colonial expansion, and impending partition, 64

Alabama affair, 51

Alexander I, Czar of Russia (1801–25), 25, 26, 28

Alexander II, Czar of Russia (1855–81), 44, 56, 58

Alexander III, Czar of Russia (1881–94), 68

Alexandria, 5, 11, 35

Anatolia, 95; German Anatolian Railways Company, 70; Turko-Italian agreement concerning Southern Anatolia, 109

Andrássy, Count Julius, Austro-Hungarian Foreign Minister (1871–1879), 62

Angora, 108

Antioch, fall of, 5

Armenia: massacres of *1895–96*, 69; Russo-Turkish compromise, 108

Athens: growth of sea power and Black Sea policy, 2–3

Austria (Holy Roman Empire) (Habsburg Monarchy): defeats Turkey *1718*, 13, 16, 19, *1699*, 18; Danube Valley surrendered by the Turks, 18; threat to Turkish monopoly of Black Sea, 18; ally of Russia in war on Turkey *1789*, 22; free passage of commercial vessels on Black Sea *1784*, 23; policy of guaranteeing existence of Turkey, 27–28, 33, 34; action by Concert of Europe proposed in aid of Turkey against Mehemet Ali, 33–35; *collective note* on the Eastern question, 34; reaction with regard to Russo-Turkish War *1877*, 56, 58, 60; Prussian-Austrian War *1866*, 58; occupation and annexation of Bosnia-Herzegovina, 58, 63, 66, 67, 77, 79, 81, 82, 85, 86, 91; original exponent of *Drang nach Osten*, 69; Triple Alliance, 66, 67; anti-Russian policy in the Near East, 69–70; Buchlau discussions with Russia regarding the Balkans, 78–79; Russian policy directed against Austria, 85, 87; *see also* Capitulations

Azof: taken by the Turks *1475*, 9; surrendered to Russia *1699*, 18; destruction of Russian forts *1739*, 19; (Azow) *1878*, 60–61

CPSIA information can be obtained at www.ICGtesting.com
Printed in the USA
BVOW05s2318201215

430700BV00008B/80/P